THE MAINE ROAD ENCYCLOPEDIA

Other titles available in the same series
The Anfield Encyclopedia: an A–Z of Liverpool FC
The Old Trafford Encyclopedia: an A–Z of Manchester United FC
The Highbury Encyclopedia: an A–Z of Arsenal FC
The Elland Road Encyclopedia: an A–Z of Leeds United FC
The Stamford Bridge Encyclopedia: an A–Z of Chelsea FC
The Maine Road Encyclopedia: an A–Z of Manchester City FC
The White Hart Lane Encyclopedia: an A–Z of Tottenham Hotspur FC
(forthcoming)
The St James's Park Encyclopedia: an A–Z of Newcastle United FC

THE
MAINE ROAD
ENCYCLOPEDIA

An A-Z of Manchester City FC

Ian Penney

Foreword by Mike Summerbee

MAINSTREAM
PUBLISHING

EDINBURGH AND LONDON

This book is dedicated to
my two godsons
Christopher Alan Yates
and
Adam John Smith
both Life Members of
the Junior Blues

Copyright © Ian Penney, 1995

The moral right of the author has been asserted

First published in Great Britain in 1995 by
MAINSTREAM PUBLISHING COMPANY
(EDINBURGH) LTD
7 Albany Street
Edinburgh EH1 3UG

ISBN 1 85158 710 1

A catalogue record for this book is available from the British
Library

Typeset in Janson by Litho Link Ltd, Welshpool, Powys, Wales
Printed and bound in Great Britain by Butler & Tanner, Frome

ACKNOWLEDGEMENTS

To my cousin Neil Woodhead, not only for his help with the research for this book, but also for carrying on the good work started by my late father in taking a youngster to Maine Road from 1966. When I was big enough to get on the Kippax wall without assistance, I used to make my own way there.

To John Maddocks, for his painstaking proof reading, assistance and grammar correction. What this man does not know about City is not worth knowing.

To Philip Noble, for providing the programme and memorabilia illustrations.

To Mike Summerbee, not only for his foreword, but also for allowing me to use the club crest.

To Joanne Parker, *News Team International* and Empics for supplying me with all the photographs.

To Karen Gibson (and Brendan), for taking over the typing of the manuscript at a crucial stage. To everyone connected with Manchester City over the last hundred years or so, without whom this book would not have been possible.

And last, but by no means least, to my wife Sheila, for putting up with me for the last twelve months as the research took over our house and, on occasion, our lives.

Ian Penney,
July 1995

FOREWORD
by Mike Summerbee

When I signed for Manchester City in August 1965, I had a feeling I might be involved in something special. Little did I know that this 'something special' would be six glorious and successful years the like of which the club has never seen, either before or since.

Those days under Joe Mercer and Malcolm Allison were the happiest of my career, and the club built up a reputation for always being friendly and welcoming. Even now, 30 years later, I am still proud of being part of a great club which last year celebrated its centenary.

This book brings back many memories for me, and probably a lot of supporters too, as it recalls the great players and occasions from the last hundred years.

As I did in 1965, I feel once again on the verge of something special. The new regime headed by Francis Lee has only the best interests of the club at heart, and we all feel sure the good times are not too far away.

Here's to another hundred years – and the memories.

Mike Summerbee

A

ABANDONED MATCHES. Since 1895, City, for various reasons, have had the misfortune to appear in 19 abandoned matches. Perhaps the most famous of these took place on 28 January 1961, when the Blues visited Luton Town for a 4th round FA Cup tie. The home side found themselves two goals in front after 18 minutes on a quagmire of a pitch. During the following 49 minutes, City and a 20-year-old Denis Law in particular, produced a magnificent display to lead 6–2. It was at this point that referee Kenny Tuck decided conditions were worsening and called the game off. The game was rearranged four days later, and in typical City style, Luton won 3–1. Denis Law scored yet again, and despite hitting the net seven times in the tie, still found himself on the losing side.

The most recent game to be abandoned was the Premier League fixture against Ipswich Town on 3 January 1994. City, languishing too close for comfort near the bottom of the league, mastered the conditions better than the visitors and deservedly led 2–0, thanks to goals from Ingebrigtsen and Vonk. With five minutes to go to half-time, and the prospects of a very welcome three points looming, the referee had no real option but to call the game off owing to the continuing monsoon which enveloped Maine Road.

ADCOCK, TONY, born Bethnal Green, 27 February 1963. Manager Mel Machin spent £85,000 on Adcock when he signed him from Colchester United on 18 June 1987. He was Machin's first signing for City, based on a scoring record of 98 goals in 210 appearances for Colchester.

Unfortunately things didn't quite work out for him at Maine Road, and he left City for Northampton Town in January the following year. During his short stay with the Blues, he did manage to reproduce his goalscoring ability, albeit for a short while, when he scored two hat-tricks in the space of four days. The first being in the 10–1 destruction of Huddersfield Town in the Second Division, the second being in the 6–2 win over Plymouth Argyle in the Simod Cup.

In total, Adcock scored nine goals in 22 appearances for City, four of which were as substitute.

AGGREGATE SCORE. City's highest aggregate scores in Cup competitions are:

COMPETITION	SCORE	OPPONENTS	SEASON	1st leg	2nd leg
League Cup	6–0	Torquay Utd	83/84	0–0 a	6–0 h
	7–3	Blackpool	84/85	4–2 h	3–1 a
	7–3	Plymouth A.	88/89	1–0 h	6–3 a
E.C.W.C.	8–0	S.K. Lierse	69/70	3–0 a	5–0 h
U.E.F.A.	5–2	A.C. Milan	78/79	2–2 a	3–0 h
Full Members Cup	3–2	Hull City	85/86	1–2 a	2–0 h

ALLEN, ALBERT, born Manchester, 16 October 1891. Moston-born full-back Bert Allen joined City in the summer of 1915, and played four senior games during the First World War. He arrived at Hyde Road from Second Division Glossop, and the first peacetime season saw him turning out regularly in the reserve side. His league debut came on 24 April 1920 in a home game against Newcastle United, and Allen was to make 56 first team appearances before being given a free transfer in 1924 to Southport. Allen later played for Crewe and Lancaster before retiring from the game in 1928. He died in Higher Blackley on 23 October 1971.

ALLEN, CLIVE, born Stepney, 20 May 1961. Although Clive Allen has played for nine different clubs, he could hardly be described as 'much travelled', as seven of these clubs have been in London. This prolific goalscorer signed for City from French side Bordeaux on 14 July 1989 for £1.1 million. He made his debut for the Blues at Anfield on 19 August that year in a game that saw City go down 3–1. In his first full season at Maine Road he equalled the top goalscoring list (11 with David White), and in total scored 21 goals in 43 (+25) appearances. For a man with such a proven goalscoring record (averaging a goal in every other game since 1978), it is hard to believe he was only capped five times for England.

Following many much publicised disagreements with player/manager Peter Reid, Clive Allen, always a favourite with the Maine Road crowd, left in December 1991, for a short stay at Stamford Bridge, before moving on across London again, this time to West Ham.

ALLISON, MALCOLM, born Dartford, 5 September 1927. Mention the name of Malcolm Allison to City fans old enough to remember the late 1960s, and one word will universally come to mind, BIG.

Long before Allison became known widely for his coaching abilities, he had himself played, with some success, at centre-half for both Charlton Athletic and West Ham United. The loss of a lung through tuberculosis in 1958 curtailed his playing career, and it was at this time that his thoughts turned to coaching.

'Big Mal' arrived at Maine Road at the request of newly appointed team manager Joe Mercer in July 1965, thus beginning the much chronicled partnership that was to dominate English football for the next few years. His route to City was by no means straightforward, stopping off as it did in such diverse places as Cambridge University, Toronto, Bath City and Plymouth Argyle.

July 1972 saw the break-up of the marvellous Mercer/Allison partnership when Joe moved on to Coventry City, leaving Malcolm now in full control of team matters at Maine Road.

In March 1973, still in his first full season as manager, Allison, angered by the Board's decision to sell Ian Mellor to Norwich City, felt he could no longer motivate the players, and left for Crystal Palace.

However, the prodigal son was to return to Maine Road in July 1979, when he again took over the manager's reigns, this time from his ex-captain Tony Book, who was given the title of general manager. Unfortunately success did not come a second time for Allison. Despite spending millions of pounds on players, City were knocked out of the FA Cup by Fourth Division Halifax Town and narrowly avoided relegation. The next season, 1980/81, proved no better, and without a win in the first twelve games, the Board decided it was time for Allison to move on again. This he did, and like nearly 20 years earlier, he travelled far and wide, from Portugal to Middlesbrough, to Kuwait to Bristol.

Whatever has been written or said about Malcolm Allison, the game will always need coaches and showmen of his calibre. Because of his successes with Joe Mercer, to this day, 'Big Mal' will always be made welcome by City fans wherever they are.

AMATEURS. Probably the first player to play in City's league side as an amateur was the legendary Billy Meredith. He signed amateur forms in October 1894, turning professional three months later.

Since Meredith, a further ten players have played in the first team as amateurs. The full list is:

Billy Meredith	1894–1895
Sam Ashworth	1903–1904
Horace Blew	1906–1907
John Willy Swann	1909–1912
George Webb	1912–1913
John Brennan	1914–1922
Stan Royle	1917–1922
Max Woosnam	1919–1925
Jim Mitchell	1922–1926
Derek Williams	1951–1955
Phil Woosnam	1951–1954

ANGLO-ITALIAN CUP. City's one and only venture into this competition took place in September 1970.

Bologna were the opposition, beating City 1–0 in Italy on 2 September, and holding the Blues to a 2–2 draw in the return leg three weeks later. City's goals were scored by George Heslop and Francis Lee.

ANGLO-SCOTTISH CUP. City have played three games in this competition, designed primarily as 'competitive' pre-season games. Despite the tournament's name, City failed to progress far enough to play north of the border. The games were:

August 2 1975 v Blackpool	(a)	0–1 Att: 11,091
August 6 1975 v Blackburn Rovers	(a)	0–1 Att: 10,612
August 9 1975 v Sheffield United	(h)	3–1 Att: 11,167

All the games were in Group One, and City's scorers were Joe Royle, Rodney Marsh and Denis Leman.

APPEARANCES. The following is a list of the top ten overall appearances for City:

	Appearances	Seasons Played
1 Alan Oakes	665 (+4)	1958–1976
2 Joe Corrigan	592	1966–1983
3 Mike Doyle	551 (+7)	1962–1978
4 Bert Trautmann	545	1949–1964
5 Eric Brook	491	1928–1940
6 Colin Bell	489 (+3)	1966–1979
7 Tommy Booth	476 (+4)	1965–1981
8 Mike Summerbee	441 (+2)	1965–1975
9 Paul Power	436 (+9)	1973–1986
10 Willie Donachie	421 (+5)	1968–1980

ARDWICK FC. Ardwick FC came into being in the summer of 1887 when finances forced Gorton AFC to look for a new ground. For the previous two seasons, Gorton had played on rented land behind The Bull's Head Hotel on Reddish Lane. At the end of the 1886/87 season, the pub landlord decided to increase the rent, and, in a situation still not unusual over a hundred years later, the club had to look closely at its books.

The captain of Gorton at this time was a Scot called K. McKenzie. McKenzie worked at a timber yard on Hyde Road, and to get to work every day he crossed an area of derelict land adjacent to some railway arches. On hearing the news that Gorton were looking for new premises, he suggested the derelict land might be suitable. First impressions did not inspire confidence as the land was no more than a cinder wreck. But on 18 June 1887, following negotiations with the land's owners, The Manchester, Sheffield and Lincolnshire Railway, Gorton secretary Walter Chew agreed a deal worth £10, to use the land for seven months.

With the new ground no longer being in Gorton, the name of the club had to change, and Ardwick FC, who joined the Football League in 1892, were to play there for the next seven years. In 1894, Ardwick became Manchester City, and they continued playing at Hyde Road until the move to Maine Road in August 1923. Although now unused, the Hyde Road Hotel still stands on its original site next door to the ground.

ASHWORTH, DAVID, born Waterford, Ireland 1868. The champions of the First Division for the 1921/22 season were Liverpool. In February 1923, when poised to win the title again, the club was shocked by the sudden resignation of its manager, David Ashworth. What made the decision even more surprising was that Ashworth left to rejoin Oldham Athletic, who were then bottom of the league. In July 1924, Ashworth arrived at Maine Road following the dismissal of Ernest Mangnall. His career with City was fairly uneventful, and in November 1925 the club accepted his resignation. That 1925/26 season saw City beaten FA Cup finalists, and relegated from Division One.

After City, Ashworth became manager of Walsall, and later scouted for Blackpool, where he passed away on 23 March 1947.

ATTENDANCES. On their way to winning the FA Cup in 1934, City entertained Stoke City in a sixth-round tie on 3 March.

*Manchester City Football Club season 1894/95: the first season of the
club since the name change from Ardwick FC
(News Team International)*

A crowd of 84,569 people packed into Maine Road to see
City win 1–0, thanks to a goal from City's all-time leading
scorer Eric Brook. This game provided a crowd the likes of
which will never be seen again; indeed, it is still a record for
any game played in England outside Wembley.

The highest attendance for a league game is 79,491 for
the Division One clash with Arsenal on 23 February 1935.
Again Brook scored, only this time the game finished 1–1.

City's lowest league attendance at Maine Road is just
8,015 for the Second Division game against Swindon Town
on 16 January 1965. The only bright spot on this desperate
afternoon was Alan Oakes's consolation goal in the 2–1
defeat.

AUSTIN, BILLY, born Arnold, Nottinghamshire, 29 April
1900. Known to the players as Sam (Samuel William), and

the fans as Billy, Austin had the misfortune to play right-wing for City following closely behind Billy Meredith.

Austin joined the Blues on 5 May 1924 from Norwich City for a fee of £2,000 plus a game at Norwich. He played a major part in City's 6–1 away win at Manchester United on 23 January 1926, when not only did he score twice, but he hit the woodwork three times. In seven seasons with City he played in 172 games, scoring 47 times, although he did miss a penalty at the end of the 1925/26 season which might have saved them from relegation. He won his one and only England cap (against Northern Ireland in 1925) whilst with City, and he was known to have deputised for injured goalkeepers on at least three different occasions.

Austin collected a Second Division Championship medal in 1928, before signing for Chesterfield on 9 December 1931. He had played only four senior games during his last three seasons at Maine Road.

B

BACUZZI, DAVE, born Islington, 12 October 1940. This England Youth International full-back played nearly five years for Arsenal before signing for City on 12 April 1964 for a fee of £14,000. Bacuzzi arrived at Maine Road at what could possibly be described as the lowest point in the club's history. Crowds of less than 11,000 were the norm at Second Division home games, and neighbours Manchester United were poised to become First Division champions.

Bacuzzi played in all except one (the first) of the games during the 1964/65 season, eventually losing his place the following season to the converted wing-half Bobby Kennedy. In total he played in 60 games for City (one as a substitute), before moving to Reading on 9 September 1966 on a free transfer.

BAKER, GRAHAM, born Southampton, 3 December 1958. City signed Baker from his home town team on 13 August 1982. He had originally been an apprentice at The Dell in 1975, and was brought to Maine Road by manager John Bond in preparation for what turned out to be a disastrous 1982/83 season.

In his first season he wore a variety of shirts in his 27 games, which saw him score just four goals. At his happiest and best when playing in midfield, Baker scored 19 times in 134 (+3) appearances for the Blues before returning to The Dell on 6 June 1987.

BALL, ALAN, born Farnworth, 12 May 1945. As the youngest member of England's World Cup winning side of 1966, Alan Ball's place in football history is assured.

His playing career had started as an amateur with Bolton Wanderers where he was released for being too small, and in September 1961 he moved to Blackpool. In May the following year he turned professional, and would score 41 times in 116 league games for the Seasiders before a British record transfer fee of £110,000 took him to Everton just 16 days after that World Cup triumph. In December 1971 Ball moved south to Arsenal for another record fee, this time £220,000.

He played over 130 league games for Arsenal before the first of his two playing spells with Southampton. These spells would be broken by his first taste of football management. On 18 February 1980 he became player/manager of Blackpool. The next few months proved less than successful for one of the game's great winners, and Ball was dismissed after just one year in charge. Within five days of his dismissal, Ball was back playing in Southampton's first team. He spent time in both Canada and Hong Kong before retiring from playing at Bristol Rovers in 1983. His career had produced 170 goals from 734 league appearances as well as 72 full England caps.

In June 1984 Ball became manager of Portsmouth where he developed some good young players. The next four-and-a-half years saw both promotion to Division One and immediate relegation. February 1989 witnessed Pompey as a struggling Second Division side, and Ball left Fratton Park to become assistant manager with Colchester United.

He moved on again in October that year, when he became assistant manager to Mick Mills at Stoke City, a position he would hold for just two weeks. During that time Mills (the man who had taken Ball on) was dismissed, and Ball was given complete control. Money spent did not produce the required goals, however, and when Stoke found themselves 14th in the Third Division (the club's lowest-ever position), they and Ball decided to part company.

After just five months out of work, Ball took over the manager's reigns at Exeter City, where he would be on the losing side in the 1992/93 Autoglass Trophy final. He stayed with Exeter until January 1994 when he returned once again to the Dell, this time as manager.

In recent times, Southampton and City have not been too dissimilar. Cash restrictions and inconsistent team performances meant both clubs have spent lengthy periods at the wrong end of the Premiership table.

Undoubtedly, however, City is by far the bigger club. It was perhaps this major factor (when coupled with the fact that Chairman Francis Lee is a longstanding friend), that persuaded Ball to leave the south coast and become City's new manager in July 1995. He would be the 15th man at City's helm since that 1966 World Cup triumph.

Both Alan Ball and Manchester City have been winners in the past. Let us all hope that this next era in the club's history will see them both winners again.

BANANAS. The inflatable bananas, such a focal point of City games at the end of the 1980s, were the brainchild of computer analyst Frank Newton. Frank began the craze in August 1987, after borrowing the original banana from a toy collector friend in Leeds.

Within a few short weeks, not only were the bananas a big hit with City fans, inflatable rivals had sprung up at other clubs the length and breadth of the country. Nicknames were the favourite, such as tigers at Hull and hammers at West Ham, but probably the funniest were the black puddings at Bury.

The high point in the bananas career had to be Saturday, 13 May 1989, the day when Trevor Morley's goal at Bradford sent City back into Division One.

BARGAIN BUYS. In these days of multi-million pound transfer fees, what constitutes a bargain buy is perhaps somewhat harder to define than in previous years, although

Brian Horton's purchase of both Paul Walsh and Uwe Rösler at the end of the 1993/94 season must certainly be classed as shrewd business to say the least.

Looking back through history, it is possible, and also a good talking point, to pick a team of bargain buys, and my own personal selection since the war is as follows:

1 Ken Mulhearn
2 Tony Book
3 Bobby McDonald
4 Bobby Kennedy
5 Dave Watson
6 Roy Paul
7 Mike Summerbee
8 Colin Bell
9 Francis Lee
10 Bobby Johnstone
11 Tony Coleman

Even allowing for inflation, this whole team can be assembled for the price of a current Premier League striker.

The ultimate bargain buy has to be home-grown talent, and with City's talent for spotting youngsters, deciding who to leave out is just as difficult as who to put in:

1 Joe Corrigan
2 Glyn Pardoe
3 Willie Donachie
4 Mike Doyle
5 Tommy Booth
6 Alan Oakes
7 Peter Barnes
8 Gary Owen
9 Neil Young
10 Stan Bowles
11 David Wagstaffe

Apologies to Messrs. Towers, Jeffries, Lake, Flitcroft, White, Brightwell, etc.

BARKAS, SAM, born Wardley, 29 December 1909. Bradford City received the princely sum of £5,000 for Barkas when he joined the Blues on 20 April 1934, and he made his debut the following month in a 3–2 defeat at Anfield.

Barkas was one of many players whose career was interrupted by war, but he remained fit enough, at 38, to captain City to the Second Division Championship in 1946/47. This Championship success made up a rare trio of medals for Barkas when added to his First Division one for City in 1936/37, and his Third Division North one, won during his days at Bradford City.

Capped five times for England, once as captain, Barkas played 191 games for City, scoring a solitary goal, against WBA in the opening game of the 1934/35 season. He left Maine Road in May 1947 to become Workington Town's manager, but was to return ten years later as a scout.

BARLOW, COLIN, born Manchester, 14 November 1935. A goalscorer for City on his debut for the club at Chelsea in the opening game of the 1957/58 season, Colin Barlow was to become an integral part of Maine Road's future 37 years later when he formed an alliance with Francis Lee to win control of Manchester City after a bitter six months power struggle with chairman Peter Swales.

A pupil of the same Collyhurst school that produced future England internationals Nobby Stiles and Brian Kidd for Manchester United, Barlow joined City as an amateur on 2 March 1956 (signed pro. in December 1956), following recommendation from scout Billy Walsh.

After his breakthrough into the senior side, Barlow became quite a prolific goalscorer for the Blues, totalling 80 in 189 league and cup appearances. The majority of these were scored from his right-wing position, although he did lead the attack on several occasions. On 30 August 1963, Barlow moved to nearby Oldham Athletic where he made just six league appearances before finishing his career with Doncaster Rovers.

Colin Barlow was a successful businessman when he joined the Francis Lee takeover group, and he became City's first managing director when the bid for control was finally successful in February 1994.

BARNES, HORACE, born Wadsley Bridge, Sheffield, 3 January 1891. As an inside-forward with a ferocious left-foot shot, Horace Barnes formed a formidable scoring partnership with Tommy Browell for several seasons both during and after World War One.

He was signed by City in May 1914 for £2,500 from Derby County, and he made his debut against Bradford City on 1 September. Barnes played 73 times for the Blues during the war, scoring an incredible 73 goals.

Such was his devotion to the club, he failed to turn up for work in a munitions factory on 29 September 1915, so he could play in a game against Stockport County. He was immediately fined for his offence by Manchester magistrates.

His scoring ability continued after the war, and in total he scored 125 times in 235 appearances for City, before moving to Preston on 11 November 1924. Even at the grand old age of 38, he was able to score 80 times for non-league Ashton National in 1928/29.

Horace Barnes passed away on 12 September 1961, although his name still lives on in Moss Side, as one of the roads near to Maine Road is named after him.

BARNES, KEN, born Birmingham, 16 March 1929. Acclaimed by many, including Denis Law, as the best uncapped wing-half ever to have played in English football, Ken Barnes joined City from Stafford Rangers on 6 May 1950. It took him until the 1954/55 season to establish himself in the first team; indeed, he had played only one senior game (against Derby County on 5 January 1952), during his first four years at Maine Road.

From that breakthrough season however, the sky-blue number four shirt belonged solely to Ken Barnes. The stylish wing-half played in both FA Cup final teams of the 50s, and almost gained that elusive international cap when he was named as reserve for The Football League against Wales in 1957.

The club's practical joker, 'Beaky' scored 19 goals in 283 games for City, including three penalties in one match – a 6–2 home win over Everton on 7 December 1957.

On 4 May 1961 Barnes became player/manager of Wrexham, where he was to stay for four years before being offered the same position at Witton Albion. For a short

Ken Barnes, described by Denis Law as 'the best uncapped wing-half ever to have played in English football'

time, Bangor City enjoyed and employed Barnes' experience, but on 27 August 1970, he returned home to Maine Road where he was appointed trainer/coach.

In 1974, Barnes, the proud father of two sons who have also worn the famous sky-blue shirt, became chief scout for the club, and was to discover several talented youngsters who would eventually make it into the first team.

Today, 45 years after his first arrival at Maine Road, Ken Barnes is still employed by Manchester City. His current job title is Assistant Chief Scout.

BARNES, PETER, born Manchester, 10 June 1957. Son of 50s favourite Ken, Peter was signed as an apprentice professional on 31 July 1972 (signed pro. July 1974). Within a short time, the jinking footwork and runs down the left wing became an invaluable part of the City sides of the mid to late 70s.

Barnes made 108 (+7) appearances and scored 15 times during his first spell at Maine Road before being transferred to WBA on 17 July 1979. During this spell, he was to win the first of his 22 England caps as well as the Young Player of the Year Award in 1976.

That same year saw Barnes score at Wembley as City beat Newcastle United to win the League Cup.

On 13 January 1987, Barnes returned to Maine Road for a second, albeit brief spell, before moving on again to Hull City in March the following year. During his 15-year playing career, Barnes played for 16 different clubs, including one in Spain and one in Portugal. Like his father, Peter is still involved with the club today. On many a rain soaked winter's evening he can be found coaching the young hopefuls at City's Platt Lane training complex.

BEAGRIE, PETER, born Middlesbrough, 29 November 1965. Manager Brian Horton obtained the services of winger Beagrie with just half an hour to go before the transfer deadline on 24 March 1994. It was coming to the end of an eventful and potentially dangerous season for the Blues, and Horton invested £1.1 million in Beagrie in an attempt to secure Premiership survival.

Beagrie had begun his career with his home town club, and had spent time with Sheffield United and Stoke City. But it was the sometimes unsettled four-and-a-half years with Everton that forced the former England Under-21 international to the forefront of the manager's mind.

Beagrie's reputation for spectacular goals, many from set pieces, and acrobatic somersaults (witnessed first hand at Maine Road when he scored twice in Everton's 5–2 victory in the last game of the 1992/93 season), will hopefully continue for many seasons whilst wearing a City shirt.

BELL, COLIN, born Hesleden, Co. Durham, 26 February 1946. As a member of the great 60s trio, Colin Bell needs no real introduction to City fans. Ironically his debut in league football was for Bury against City in a 1–1 draw at Maine Road on 8 February 1964. A further irony was that Colin Bell scored Bury's goal that day.

Arguably the best City player of all time, Colin Bell. With 48 caps, he is the most capped player ever to be on the club's books
(News Team International)

After considerable persuasion, Manager Joe Mercer was finally convinced by Malcolm Allison and Chief Scout Harry Godwin that City should sign the player later nicknamed 'Nijinsky'. £45,000 secured Bell's signature on 16 March 1966, and he made his debut three days later in a 2–1 win at Derby County. Again Bell scored, although this time with a part of the body not normally associated with goalscoring.

As a member of the side that won almost everything over the next few years, Bell's contribution was immeasurable. Often compared to the great Peter Doherty, Bell was perhaps the most complete player ever at Maine Road.

He was to play twice for England Under-23s, before gaining the first of his 48 full caps against Sweden on 22 May 1968.

On 12 November 1975, Bell suffered a serious knee injury in a tackle with Manchester United's Martin Buchan, during a League Cup tie which the Blues won 4–0. Bell was then only 29, and a career which would have gone on both at club and international level for many years, was effectively curtailed.

City's most capped international and sixth placed in the overall appearances table tried manfully to regain full fitness, but could unfortunately never quite manage it. He was finally forced to retire from the game on 21 August 1979.

During his time as a player with City, Bell scored 152 goals in 489 (+3) appearances, and he returned to Maine Road in 1990 as reserve/youth team coach. One of England's greatest ever footballers is today passing on advice to young Blues in his capacity as youth development officer.

BENNETT, DAVID, born Manchester, 11 July 1959. David Bennett was one of two locally born brothers who joined City in the second half of the 1970s. Signed from Ashford Celtic on 26 November 1976, Bennett's debut came as a substitute in a goalless draw with Everton on 14 April 1979.

A skilful if slight forward, Bennett established himself in the first team the following season, and went on to make 55 (+10) league and cup appearances, scoring 15 times, before being transferred to Cardiff City on 17 September 1981. The peak of his Maine Road career had come earlier that year, when he played in both the FA Cup final and replay against Tottenham Hotspur. In the replay Bennett himself was brought down in the penalty area allowing Kevin Reeves to give City the lead, before the Blues fell victims to the Spurs' Ricky Villa-inspired comeback.

Following Cardiff, Bennett played for Coventry City, where he was to avenge that Cup final defeat in 1987, as the Midlanders triumphed 3–2 over Spurs.

BENSON, JOHN, born Arbroath, 23 December 1942. Wing-half John Benson signed professional forms for City in July 1961 after being signed as an amateur three years earlier from Stockport Boys. Benson was to play 52 times for City over the next three seasons, finally losing his regular spot to Bobby Kennedy, before moving to Torquay United for £5,000 on 15 June 1964. After 233 (+7) league games for Torquay, Benson moved along the south coast to Bournemouth, and for the first time, was to join forces with John Bond.

Early in the 1980/81 season, Benson returned to Maine Road as assistant manager to Bond, continuing a managerial partnership formed initially at Norwich City in 1973.

Following Bond's resignation in February 1983, Benson gained full control at Maine Road, but was to leave the club less than four months later after City were relegated to Division Two.

BETTS, BARRIE, born Barnsley, 18 September 1932. Barrie Betts arrived at Maine Road on 24 June 1960 from neighbours Stockport County for a fee of £8,000. His career had started at Barnsley, where he suffered a serious back injury, and his first season in the top flight saw him captain the Blues, play in all 42 league games, and win City's Player of the Year Award.

He formed a regular full-back combination with Welsh international Cliff Sear, and was to play in 117 games for City, scoring six goals, four of which were in that first season.

On 12 August 1964, Betts was given a free transfer to Scunthorpe United, where he was forced to retire through injury after playing only seven league games.

BISHOP, IAN, born Liverpool, 29 May 1965. Although he played only 22 league and cup games in his five-month stay with City, Ian Bishop was firmly established as a Maine Road favourite.

Signed by manager Mel Machin for £465,000 from Second Division Bournemouth on 7 July 1989, Bishop made his debut along with Clive Allen in the 3–1 defeat at Anfield on 19 August.

Before Bournemouth, Bishop had played at Carlisle, Crewe and originally Everton, in 1983, when Howard Kendall was manager. Following Kendall's arrival at Maine Road in December 1989, Bishop's outings were limited to just one appearance as substitute, and he left City, with Trevor Morley, in that same month, in a deal that would take them to West Ham and bring Mark Ward to Maine Road.

It has been suggested that Kendall's alleged prejudice against long hair was instrumental in the transfer, but, whatever the reason, Bishop will always be remembered by City fans not only for his passing ability, but also for his tremendous diving header in the famous 5–1 win over United.

BLACK, ANDREW, born Stirling, 23 September 1917. Capped three times for Scotland, inside-forward Andy Black first tasted English football during World War Two, when, as a PE instructor, he had guested for Crewe, Chester, Grimsby, York, Portsmouth, Aldershot and Liverpool.

After playing eleven seasons for Hearts, Black signed for City on 6 June 1946, making his debut at Leicester on 31 August in a game City won 3–0. That season saw City win the Second Division Championship, and Black was leading scorer the following year with 16 goals in 37 games.

In total he scored 53 times in 146 appearances for City before moving to Stockport County on 3 August 1950, where he scored a further 38 goals in 94 league matches.

BLUE MOON 'Blue Moon, you saw me standing alone', is the opening line of the unofficial anthem of Manchester City Football Club.

Unashamedly stolen from the song written by Richard Rodgers and Lorenz Hart, *Blue Moon*, has been a feature of all City games over the last few years, whether during a lull in play, or to celebrate a goal.

BOND, JOHN, born Colchester, 17 December 1932. As a player, John Bond enjoyed seventeen seasons in league football, with both West Ham and Torquay United. Whilst at Upton Park in the 50s, he had played in the same side as another future City manager, Malcolm Allison.

Bond took over from Allison when he arrived at a struggling Maine Road in October 1980, to inherit a City side without a win in their first twelve games. Changes obviously had to be made, and amongst Bond's first signings were the vastly experienced Tommy Hutchison, Gerry Gow and Bobby McDonald.

Stability and respectability were eventually achieved in that first season (finishing 12th in the league), which also saw the Blues beaten in the League Cup semi-final by Liverpool, and by Tottenham in the replayed FA Cup final.

Further signings of the calibre of Trevor Francis and Asa Hartford followed, and City finished tenth the next season, after a start which had promised greater things.

At the start of the 1982/83 season, Bond and his assistant John Benson, turned down an offer of employment from Portuguese giants Benfica. By January 1983, Bond must have wished he had taken that offer as City crashed out of the FA Cup 4–0 at Brighton.

He resigned shortly afterwards, and has since managed Burnley (where he proved unpopular), Swansea, Birmingham City and Shrewsbury Town.

BOND, KEVIN, born West Ham, 22 June 1957. Kevin Bond played 122 (+2) games for City after being signed from American side Seattle Sounders on 7 September 1981.

Thought by many to be in the side only because his father was manager, Bond junior weathered these initial misgivings, so much so in fact that he was voted the Supporters' Player of the Year for the 1982/83 season.

Bond started his career as an apprentice with Bournemouth before moving to Norwich in July 1974, again where his father was in charge. Following a year in the States, this central-defender made his debut for the Blues at right-back in a 3–0 defeat at Birmingham on 19 September 1981.

On 24 September 1984, Bond left Maine Road for Southampton, where he was to stay for nearly four years before returning to Bournemouth in August 1988.

BOOK, TONY, born Bath, 4 September 1935.

On 20 July 1966, Joe Mercer, prompted by an enthusiastic Malcolm Allison, spent £17,000 on a 30-year-old full-back, who two years earlier, had been sharing his

Tony Book, City's most successful captain, proudly displays the 1970 European Cup Winners' Cup on the Blues' return to Manchester Airport (News Team International)

time between playing part-time football with Bath City and bricklaying.

Tony Book had left Bath for Plymouth Argyle (both clubs managed by Allison), for whom he was to play 81 times before arriving at Maine Road. He missed only one game in his first two seasons, but the start of the 1968/69 season threw doubts on any future he may have had in top flight football.

Book was out of action for 25 games with an Achilles tendon injury, but within six months of his return, he was lifting the FA Cup at Wembley, and sharing the Footballer of the Year Award with Derby County's Dave Mackay. These awards were additional to his Championship medal won twelve months earlier.

Further medals and triumphs were to follow for 'The Skipper', who played 306 (+3) games before retiring on 30 November 1973. However, that was not the end of Tony Book's association with Manchester City.

He became assistant manager to Ron Saunders in 1973, taking over the manager's reins the following year. In 1976 he took City to Wembley triumph again, this time with a 2–1 League Cup win over Newcastle United. The Blues finished runners-up in 1976/77, and Book was to build a strong and talented squad around players such as Dave Watson, Joy Royle and Mike Channon, before Allison's return to Maine Road in July 1979.

Apart from a six month spell in an advisory capacity at Cardiff City in 1981, Tony Book has remained at Maine Road for 29 years. During that time he has had numerous varied roles apart from those already mentioned. These include youth development officer, general manager, and reserve team coach, and he is presently first team coach.

BOOKS. It is a great tragedy that, over the years, the publishing world has seen fit to produce countless books on one Manchester club at the expense of the other.

Obviously in compiling a work of this nature, many books have been consulted, ranging from player biographies to reference and yearbooks. A full bibliography appears on page 221.

It is hoped that this publication will go some way to redress this obvious imbalance.

BOOTH, TOMMY, born Manchester, 9 November 1949. City's legendary manager Joe Mercer once said of Tommy Booth; 'He is the best footballing centre-half since Stan Cullis'.

Praise indeed for a young Langley lad who signed professional forms for the Blues on 26 August 1967, having been on the club's books as an amateur since September 1965.

Booth made his first team debut on 2 September 1968 in a goalless League Cup tie at Huddersfield. Such was the impression left on Mercer that the 18-year-old's league debut, against the might of Arsenal, was to come just over a month later, on 9 October.

He was to play in 28 of the remaining 30 league games that season, so deposing George Heslop from the number five position. In just over thirteen seasons with City, Booth played in 476 (+4) games, putting him in seventh place in the overall appearances tables.

During that time, he scored 36 goals, some from a midfield position he was to adopt later in his career, but the most important one has to be his winner against Everton in the 1969 FA Cup semi-final.

The holder of four England Under-23 caps, Booth moved to Preston on 4 October 1981 for a fee of £30,000, where he was manager for a short spell in the 1985/86 season.

BOWLES, STAN, born Manchester, 24 December 1948. Stan Bowles actually made his mark as an international class footballer long after he had left Maine Road, but it was City who discovered and nurtured one of the great natural talents of his era.

Moston born, Bowles made a dramatic introduction to senior football with four goals in his first one-and-a-half games. Coming on as a substitute in a League Cup win over Leicester City on 13 September 1967, Bowles scored twice, and, just three days later, he scored two more, this time on his league debut, a 5–2 victory over Sheffield United.

A rebellious streak however led to frequent clashes with both Joe Mercer and Malcolm Allison, and on one occasion he mysteriously disappeared for a short while after missing the plane for a friendly against Ajax in Amsterdam. Problems in his personal life caused City to finally lose patience with their wayward young genius, and on 22 September 1970, after a brief loan spell at Bury, Bowles signed for Crewe Alexandra. He had made just 16 (+4) appearances in a City shirt.

Unable to settle also at Crewe, Bowles left the north west completely in October 1971, when he moved to Carlisle United. At Brunton Park his undoubted talents blossomed, and he was targeted by Queens Park Rangers, where he spent seven seasons, scoring 70 goals in 255 league appearances.

This period was the pinnacle of Bowles' career, and although he was by now one of the game's most famous names, his reputation and flamboyant style of play earned him only five England caps.

Bowles later played for Nottingham Forest, Leyton Orient and Brentford, but left the impression of an enormous talent that perhaps never quite reached the heights it could have done.

BOWYER, IAN, born Ellesmere Port, 6 June 1951. This former mid-Cheshire boys player originally signed for City on apprentice forms on 30 July 1966, when he was just fifteen. In November 1968, injuries forced the Blues to give Bowyer his first team chance, and he made his debut in a 1–0 defeat at Newcastle. He played only a handful of games that season, but he did play in 33 (+1) games the following season, when he replaced the injured Neil Young after the opening game.

Despite scoring six times in his first eight outings, Bowyer was given a particularly hard time by certain sections of the crowd, and he eventually left Maine Road for Leyton Orient on 11 June 1971. In October 1973, Brian Clough took Bowyer to Nottingham Forest, where, in two spells, he was to play in nearly 600 games, collecting on his way, two European Cup Winners' medals, to go alongside the League Cup and European Cup Winners' Cup medals won during his time at Maine Road.

BRANAGAN, KEN, born Salford, 27 July 1930. Full-back Ken Branagan arrived at Maine Road from North Salford Youth Club on 5 November 1948. National Service prevented him from making his first team debut for a further two years, until 9 December 1950, in a spectacular 5–3 home victory against Sheffield United.

Over the next few seasons, this former Boys' Club international, was to become City's regular right-back, eventually losing out to Bill Leivers in December 1955, so costing him a place in the winning 1956 FA Cup final team. The unfortunate Branagan had previously lost his spot in 1955 to Jimmy Meadows, so missing out in that year's final as well, when he had his appendix removed.

Branagan was to play a total of 208 games for the Blues, scoring just three times, before moving, along with team-mate

Bert Lister, to Oldham Athletic on 1 October 1960. He made 177 league appearances for Latics, returning to Boundary Park in 1973 as reserve team trainer, and was fortunate enough to watch his son Jim play league football for teams such as Blackburn Rovers and York City.

BRAY, JACKIE, born Oswaldtwistle, 22 April 1909. Manchester Central were the recipients of £1,000 from Manchester City in October 1929 for the services of left-half Jackie Bray. Following a short spell in Central League football, Bray's first team debut came in the heat of a Manchester derby, a 1–0 defeat at Old Trafford on 8 February 1930. His speed and ability on the ball established him in the senior side for the next nine years, until, as with many other players of the time, his career was cut short by the outbreak of war.

Bray was an important member of the successful City sides of the 30s, earning an FA Cup runners'-up medal in 1933, and a winners' one the following year. In addition to his 1937 Championship medal, Bray was also the recipient of six full international caps, and played five times for the Football League.

After nine reserve team games of City's Second Division Championship season 1946/47, the 37-year-old Bray left Maine Road to become manager at Watford. He was to spend a short time as coach at Nelson before retiring from the game in 1948.

BRIGHTWELL, DAVID, born Lutterworth, 7 January 1971. Son of Britain's famous 60s athletes Anne Packer and Robbie Brightwell, this 6ft 2in left-sided player is best suited to central defence, but he has played left-back and dual attacker since making his first team debut as substitute at Wimbledon on 22 February 1992. His first full game was as replacement for Steve Redmond seven days later in a 2–0 home win against Aston Villa.

The youngest of the Brightwell brothers signed professional forms for City after leaving school in April 1988, and gained League experience whilst on loan to Third Division Chester City in March 1991.

THE MAINE ROAD ENCYCLOPEDIA

A regular on the substitutes' bench of late, manager Brian Horton gave him an extended run at left-back towards the end of the 1993/94 season. David Brightwell was to repay his manager's faith in him with some fine performances, and a crucial winning goal against Newcastle United on 9 April 1994, his first for the club.

BRIGHTWELL, IAN, born Lutterworth, 9 April 1968. With such famous and talented parents, it was a reasonably safe assumption that, as a schoolboy, Ian Brightwell would be able to run. This indeed he could, at both 400 and 800 metres, but athletics' loss was football's gain, when Ian signed associate schoolboy forms for City in September 1982.

On 3 May 1986, he turned professional, and was a member of the excellent City side that won the FA Youth Cup that year. Like his younger brother David, he too made his debut against Wimbledon, this time on 23 August 1986. His first senior goal was scored in the 1–1 draw at Norwich on 14 February 1987, and once established in the first team squad, he has become the club's utility man, although he is perhaps at his best when playing at right-back.

A serious knee injury sustained in an FA Cup tie at Reading in January 1993 forced him out of the game for what was to be fourteen long months. Brightwell had three operations before returning to first team duty, as a midfielder this time, in the goalless draw at Oldham on 26 March 1994. This match also proved to be the first time both Brightwell brothers had started a senior game together.

Already an England representative at Schoolboy, Youth and Under-21 levels, it is now surely only a matter of time before a fully fit Brightwell goes on to gain further international honours.

BROADIS, IVOR, born Isle of Dogs, 18 December 1922. Whilst serving with the RAF during World War Two, Ivor Broadis was to guest as an amateur with Millwall, Bradford Park Avenue, Manchester United, Tottenham Hotspur and Carlisle United. Carlisle were so impressed with the then

23-year-old Broadis that they offered him the position of player/manager in August 1946.

In February 1949, Broadis caused something of a stir when he transferred himself to Sunderland for £19,000.

On 5 October 1951, manager Les McDowall broke the club's transfer record when City paid Sunderland £25,000 for this fast and fierce shooting inside-forward. Within two months of his arrival at Maine Road, Broadis was winning the first of his fourteen England caps, in the 2–2 draw with Austria at Wembley.

Broadis moved back to the north east, this time to Newcastle United, on 29 October 1953, and was to play against the Blues in the 1955 FA Cup Final.

During his time at Maine Road, Broadis played in 79 games and scored 12 goals. A second spell with Carlisle followed Newcastle, and then a move to Queen of the South, before he finally retired to become a successful football journalist.

BROOK, ERIC, born Mexborough, 27 November 1907. 177 goals in 491 games make Eric Brook City's all-time leading goalscorer, and place him fifth in the appearances table.

Along with Freddie Tilson, Brook was a £6,000 double signing from Barnsley on 16 March 1928, making his debut against Grimsby Town the following day. Although officially an outside-left, Brook was given a licence to roam, and would often appear in the centre-forward position where he scored many fine goals over the years.

He scored six times on City's route to Wembley in 1933, where he became the first player to wear the number twelve shirt in a Cup Final. (In that game, the players were numbered 1 to 22. Everton 1 to 11, and City, outside-left first, 12 to 22.)

Brook's goal, this time a centre from the left wing, decided a Cup tie the following season, when a record 84,569 crowded into Maine Road for the sixth round game against Stoke City. He also deputised for injured goalkeepers on at least three occasions, and in all four of England's internationals during the 1933/34 season, he scored in every one.

Eric Brook played 18 times for England, where the ferocity and accuracy of his shooting also made him the regular penalty taker. He played in all three league games in the war-shortened 1939/40 season, but injuries received in a car crash were to finish his career. He died in March 1965, aged 57, and at the time of writing, it is impossible to say who will get near his achievements for City, let alone overtake them.

BROTHERS. To date, a total of sixteen different sets of brothers have played for City. They are:

	From		To	
BARNES, Peter	Jul.	72	Jul.	79
	Jan.	87	Mar.	88
BARNES, Mike	Apr.	77	cs	79
BECKFORD, Darren	Apr.	84	Jun.	87
BECKFORD, Jason	Jul.	86	Jan.	92
BENNETT, Dave	Nov.	76	Sep.	81
BENNETT, Gary	Sep.	79	Jul.	81
BRIGHTWELL, Ian	May	86	Present	
BRIGHTWELL, David	Apr.	88	Present	
BROAD, Jimmy	Nov.	09	Oct.	10
	Sep.	12	Aug.	13
BROAD, Tommy	Mar.	19	May	21
CATON, Tommy	Jul.	79	Nov.	83
CATON, Paul	Sep.	83	May	84
COOKSON, Sammy	Oct.	18	Sep.	28
COOKSON, Jimmy	Sep.	20	Jul.	25
CORBETT, Frank	Mar.	30	Jul.	36
CORBETT, Vic	May	33	May	35
CUNLIFFE, Bobby	Jul.	60	Jun.	65
CUNLIFFE, David	Jul.	66	Nov.	69
DORSETT, George	Dec.	04	cs	12
DORSETT, Joe	Aug.	10	Jun.	20
FAIRCLOUGH, Albert	Apr.	13	cs	20
FAIRCLOUGH, Peter	Apr.	13	Aug.	20
FUTCHER, Paul	Jun.	78	Jul.	80
FUTCHER, Ron	Aug.	78	Apr.	79
HYNDS, Tom	Sep.	01	Dec.	06
HYNDS, John	Sep.	10	cs	11

LAKE, Paul	Jul. 85	Present	
LAKE, Mike	Sep. 85	Reserve trialist	
LAKE, Dave	May 88	Reserve trialist	
MOFFATT, Robert	Aug. 1895	cs	07
MOFFATT, James	May 03	cs	06
ROSS, Frank	Jun. 47	Feb. 48	
ROSS, George	Jun. 47	Dec. 47	

BROWELL, TOMMY, born Walbottle, Northumberland, 19 October 1892. Hull City already had two Browell brothers on their books in 1910, but such was their determination to sign Tommy, that directors rowed across the Tyne to reach the coalmining village where he lived, and they agreed terms in his mother's cottage.

In October 1910, Tommy, still only 18, scored a hat-trick for Hull against Stockport County. A journalist reported that 'ten men and a boy beat Stockport', and Browell was to keep the nickname 'Boy' throughout his playing career.

His scoring ability soon attracted the big clubs, one of which was Everton, who were to pay £1,650 for him in December 1911.

Almost two years later, on 31 October 1913, Browell arrived at Hyde Road for a fee of £1,780. He continued his superb goalscoring feats in City's colours, and his 139 goals in 247 games place him seventh in the club's all time goalscoring table.

Despite this goalscoring prowess, Browell was unfortunate never to play for his country, and on 15 September 1926 he left City to join Blackpool, staying on in the resort after his playing career had finished.

Tommy Browell became a tram driver, before passing away on 5 October 1955, just days before his 63rd birthday.

BUSBY, SIR MATT, born Orbiston, 26 May 1909. It has probably been forgotten by many, if indeed known at all, that the man who became a legend at Old Trafford was actually introduced to English football by Manchester City.

It was February 1928, and the seventeen-year-old Busby and his widowed mother were all set to emigrate to the

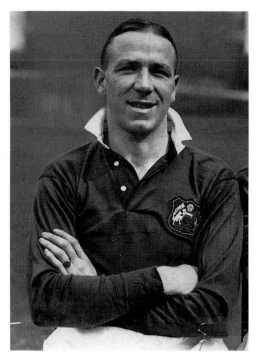

The late Sir Matt Busby – discovered by one Manchester club, only to become a legend at the other (News Team International)

United States. Having played for three Scottish non-league sides, Busby's abilities as an inside-forward had been brought to the attention of City's manager Peter Hodge.

The prospect of a slap-up meal in a Glasgow restaurant, the regal wage of £5 per week, and some delicate negotiations with Mrs Busby, enabled Hodge finally to force Busby south instead of west.

Busby's debut for City came in a 3–1 home victory over Middlesbrough on 2 November 1929. He played eleven times that season, always in an inside-forward position, but manager Hodge was to switch him to wing-half for the start of the 1930/31 season, and this proved to be his best position.

In total he made 226 appearances for City, scoring 14 times, before moving to Anfield on 11 March 1936 for a fee of £8,000. During his time at Maine Road, Busby played in two FA Cup finals, won his one and only Scottish cap (against Wales in 1933), and was almost bought as a player by Manchester United. The miserly offer of £150 quite rightly being dismissed by Hodge.

His playing career was curtailed by the outbreak of World War Two, and following his army service, he finally arrived at Old Trafford, this time as manager, in 1945. His salary at the time was reported to have been £15 per week. The rest, as they say, is history.

Sir Matt Busby, undoubtedly one of football's greatest ambassadors, died after a short illness, on 20 January 1994. He was 84.

C

CAPS. The following players have all won full international caps during their playing careers with Manchester City. The numbers shown do not include caps won whilst playing for any other club.

ENGLAND (33)

AUSTIN, Billy	1
BARKAS, Sam	5
BARNES, Peter	14
BELL, Colin	48
BOOTH, Frank	1
BRAY, Jackie	6
BROADIS, Ivor	8
BROOK, Eric	18
BURGESS, Herbert	4
CHANNON, Mike	1
CORRIGAN, Joe	9
COWAN, Sam	3
CURLE, Keith	3
DOYLE, Mike	5
FRANCIS, Trevor	10
JOHNSON, Tommy	2
LEE, Francis	27

SCOTLAND (10)

BUSBY, Matt	1
DONACHIE, Willie	35
HARTFORD, Asa	36
JOHNSTONE, Bobby	4
LAW, Denis	11
LIVINGSTONE, George	1
McLUCKIE, Jimmy	1
McMULLAN, Jimmy	8
PLENDERLEITH, Jackie	1
STEWART, George	2

WALES (17)

CHAPMAN, Tom	2
CLARKE, Roy	22
DAVIES, Gordon	3

MARSH, Rodney	8	DAVIES, Joe	3
MEADOWS, Jimmy	1	DAVIES, Wyn	3
MITCHELL, Jim	1	DIBBLE, Andy	3
REEVES, Kevin	1	GRAY, Albert	5
REVIE, Don	6	HUGHES, Edwin	3
ROBERTS, Frank	4	JONES, Di	2
ROYLE, Joe	4	JONES, Willy Lot	18
SPROSTON, Bert	1	LEWIS, William	2
SUMMERBEE, Mike	8	MEREDITH, Billy	22
SWIFT, Frank	19	MORRIS, Hugh	1
THORNLEY, Irvine	1	PAUL, Roy	24
TILSON, Fred	4	PHILLIPS, David	10
TUEART, Dennis	6	SEAR, Cliff	1
WATSON, Dave	30	WYNN, George	8
WHITE, David	1		
WOOSNAM, Max	1		

NORTHERN IRELAND (14) and Ireland before 1924

REPUBLIC OF IRELAND (8)

		CONWAY, Jimmy	1
CROSSAN, Johnny	10	DUNNE, Leo	2
DOHERTY, Peter	6	FAGAN, Fionan 'Paddy'	2
FLEMING, Gary	2	KERNAGHAN, Alan	6
HAMILL, Mickey	1	McCARTHY, Mick	22
HUGHES, Michael	4	PHELAN, Terry	18
KELLY, Patrick	1	QUINN, Niall	38
LOMAS, Steve	6	WALSH, William	9
McADAMS, Bill	5		
McCOURT, Frank	6		
McCULLOUGH, Keillor	3		
McILROY, Sammy	10	NORWAY (2)	
MULLIGAN, Jimmy	1		
O'NEILL, Martin	1	HAREIDE, Aage	9
WALSH, William	5	INGEBRIGTSEN, Kaare	1

CATON, Tommy, born Liverpool, 6 October 1962. Centre-half Tommy Caton signed apprentice forms for City on 5 July 1979. This must have been a difficult decision for him, as he was wanted by both Manchester clubs, and by both his hometown clubs. As all City fans know, however, there was only one real team to sign for, and the 16-year-old Caton made his league debut for the Blues in the opening game of the 1979/80 season (0–0 at home to Crystal Palace).

The newly appointed manager Malcolm Allison was so impressed by the youngster, that he played Caton in all 42 league games that season. Incidentally, at that time, Caton was also captaining the youth side. On his seventeenth birthday, Caton turned professional, and would later play in both games of the 1981 FA Cup final. These appearances when added to his FA Youth Cup final appearances for City, meant that he had played in four Cup finals before turning 19. Unfortunately for Caton, he came away with runners' up medals every time.

In 197 (+1) appearances for City, Caton scored 8 goals, before a £500,000 transfer took him to Arsenal on 30 November 1983. His reluctance to play Second Division football was the reason for this move, and it was hoped that Arsenal could finally provide the springboard needed for Caton to win full international honours. However this proved not to be, and he was to retire from the game in 1993 after repeated foot operations, content only with England Youth and Under-21 caps.

In April that same year, the 30-year-old Caton was to die tragically of a heart attack at his Oxfordshire home.

CENTENARY. Manchester City Football Club celebrated their centenary year in 1994. In March 1894, Ardwick FC, after a reasonable start to the season, found themselves hurtling into oblivion. A run of heavy defeats, a mass exodus of players, severe financial difficulties and re-election preceded the announcement in the *Manchester Evening Mail* on 21 April of 'a new company, Manchester City'.

This new company was the brainchild of the Ardwick secretary Joshua Parlby, and just over four months later, on 1 September 1894, Manchester City played their first game in league football.

A crowd of around 7,000 saw City lose 4–2 at nearby Bury, but that first season was to be memorable in many ways.

As well as the formation of the new club, the legendary Billy Meredith arrived at the still used Hyde Road ground, and City had an 11–3 victory over Lincoln City (on 23 March 1895). In terms of goals scored, that win still stands today as City's highest ever league victory.

CENTRAL LEAGUE. Since the 1892/93 season, City (or Ardwick), have fielded a reserve side in addition to the first team. From that first season, until the end of the 1910/11 season, City's reserves played in the Lancashire Combination. During those 19 years, the Blues came out winners twice, and runners-up twice.

In 1911/12, City joined the Central League on its formation, but it wasn't until the 1977/78 season that they managed to win the title. Their previous best being fourth, a position they achieved five times, and were to achieve again the year after their Championship success.

Owing to their final position of 18th in the 1981/82 season, City found themselves relegated to the newly formed Division Two of the Central League. Within the space of one season, they had bounced back to the First Division. At the end of the 1983/84 season, the Blues found themselves once again, finishing in fourth place.

CHAMPIONSHIP. Unfortunately, for a club of City's stature and following, the First Division Championship has only visited the Blues twice this century.

The first time was in the 1936/37 season, when City scored an amazing 107 goals, with Doherty and Brook providing 50 of these goals between them. In typical Blues fashion, they were relegated the following season.

It was to be a further 31 years, until that famous 4–3 victory at St. James' Park on 11 May 1968, before the title returned to Maine Road. City have managed the runners'-up spot on three occasions, 1903/04, 1920/21, and 1976/77.

City have faired better in their pursuit of the Second Division title. This they have managed to win on six occasions, the last time being when Johnny Crossan skippered the triumphant Blues in the 1965/66 season. Their previous successes were 1898/99, 1902/03, 1909/10, 1926/27 and 1946/47.

THE MAINE ROAD ENCYCLOPEDIA

CHANNON, MIKE, born Orcheston, 28 November 1948. Mike Channon was seen as the final cog in a City team poised to win the League Championship when he arrived at Maine Road for £300,000 from Southampton on 25 July 1977. He was already an established England international forward after eleven years on the south coast, where he had picked up an FA Cup winners' medal in 1976, and he joined a City side that had lost out on the title by only one point to Liverpool the previous season. The mix seemed irresistible. Unfortunately, however, it didn't quite work out like that. Although Channon scored 30 goals in his 91 (+3) league and cup appearances, many memorable only for the windmill which followed, he never really reproduced his very best form for City. He added only one more England cap to his collection during his stay at Maine Road, before returning to his first love Southampton on 8 September 1979 for a fee of £250,000.

The now successful racehorse owner had spells with Newcastle United, Bristol Rovers, Norwich City and Portsmouth, before finally retiring in 1985.

CHARITY SHIELD. To date, City have appeared in seven FA Charity Shield matches, being successful on three occasions.

The victories were in:
1937 2–0 v Sunderland at Maine Road (Herd, Doherty)
1968 6–1 v WBA at Maine Road (Lee 2, Owen 2, Young, Opp own goal)
1972 1–0 v Aston Villa at Villa Park (Lee)

The defeats were in:
1934 4–0 v Arsenal at Highbury
1956 1–0 v Manchester United at Maine Road
1969 2–1 v Leeds United at Elland Road (Bell)
1973 1–0 v Burnley at Maine Road

CHEETHAM, ROY, born Manchester, 2 December 1939. A former Manchester Boys player, Eccles born Roy Cheetham signed for City as an amateur on 30 June 1956. Within six months, professional terms had been negotiated, but Cheetham had to wait until 8 March 1958 for his first team debut, a 2–1 away win over Luton Town.

Over the next ten years, the ever dependable right-half was to play only 138 (+5) games for the Blues, but gained the reputation of being a tremendous club servant, whether or not he was in the first team. His obvious loyalty to City can be seen in his record 218 appearances for the reserves.

Cheetham played in only three games of the Championship season, and on 2 January 1968, he moved to the United States, where he played ten months with the Detroit Cougars. He returned to England in October 1968 for a short spell with Charlton Athletic, before spending the last three seasons of his career with Chester.

CLARKE, ROY, born Newport, 1 June 1925. Roy 'Nobby' Clarke came from a Welsh mining family and worked as a Bevin Boy during World War Two.

A Welsh schoolboy baseball international, Clarke's football career took off in the 1946/47 season, as a goalscoring winger in Cardiff City's promotion winning side. At the end of that season, Clarke was involved in a unique treble which saw him play in three different divisions of the Football League in three consecutive games.

He played for Cardiff in their penultimate match in the Third Division, then on 23 May 1947, he joined City for £12,000, just in time to make his debut in the final fixture of the Blues' Second Division Championship winning campaign. His next game therefore, was in the First Division, in City's opening game of the 1947/48 season.

In more than eleven years at Maine Road, Clarke scored many vital goals, none more so than in the 1955 FA Cup semi-final at Villa Park, when, in mudbath conditions, his diving header earned the Blues a 1–0 victory over the fancied Sunderland. Joy changed to despair, however, when minutes later, Clarke was carried off with a knee injury which would eventually cause him to miss the final.

That was a typical slice of the bad luck which dogged Roy Clarke's City career. Although he won an FA Cup winners'

medal in 1956 and clocked up 369 league and cup
appearances, with 79 goals, he would have played in many
more games had it not been for a catalogue of various
injuries and ailments.

Clarke won 22 Welsh international caps whilst at Maine
Road, and was rewarded with a £1,000 benefit cheque for
ten years' service in 1957.

On 19 September 1958, he moved to Stockport County
for £1,500 but later returned to Maine Road to serve his
beloved City in a variety of backroom roles over the years.

CLEMENTS, KENNY, born Manchester, 9 April 1955.
Kenny Clements was performing ground staff duties for the
Blues in July 1975 when City thought he might be better
employed as a player.

He was given his first team chance, along with Paul
Power, in a 1–0 defeat at Villa Park on 27 August that year.
Although Clements wore the number two shirt during his
first spell at Maine Road, his physical presence and heading
ability caused concern in many an opposition goalmouth.

On 12 September 1979, £250,000 took Clements to
Oldham Athletic, where he was used mainly as a central
defender. 9 March 1985 saw Clements' second debut for
City (and third broken nose), in a 1–0 home victory against
Middlesbrough.

After 275 (+7) appearances, with two goals, Clements
moved to Bury on 17 March 1988. He played 66 (+15)
league games for Bury before spending time at Limerick
City and Shrewsbury Town.

COLEMAN, TONY, born Liverpool, 2 May 1945. Despite
reservations by Joe Mercer, Malcolm Allison wanted to sign
a 21-year-old left-winger with a reputation as a potential
trouble-maker.

Tony Coleman, a former ice-cream man, was this player,
playing at the time for Third (soon to be Fourth) Division
Doncaster Rovers. Allison was convinced that Coleman's
efforts and energy could be harnessed for the good of the
Blues, and on 16 March 1967, £12,350 changed hands, and
'T.C.' became a City player.

Over the next three seasons, the familiar blond figure, with the habit of holding his shirt cuffs tightly in his fingers, was a fearsome sight for opposing right-backs. During his time at Maine Road, Coleman played in 101 (+2) games for City, scoring 16 times, but providing many more for the other members of that great forward line.

With City he won League Championship and FA Cup winners' medals, before being sold to Sheffield Wednesday on 1 October 1969 for £14,000.

Now living in Australia, Tony Coleman will always be remembered by City fans for his remark to Princess Anne prior to the 1969 FA Cup final – 'Give my regards to your mum and dad.'

COLOURS. The many books consulted during the compiling of this encyclopedia, have proved largely fruitless with regard to colours.

Having said that, however, early newspaper reports claim that Gorton wore a black shirt with a large white cross on the front. The kit being donated at the time by the local parish, hence the cross. In 1887/88, Ardwick's kit was described as 'white shirts with white knickerbockers', whilst Manchester City's first season 1894/95 saw them wearing 'Cambridge Blue jerseys with grey shorts'.

Two seasons later, 1896/97, 'Cambridge Blue jerseys with white shorts' became City's regular kit. Some cynics at the time said that these white shorts were in fact the old grey ones which had been washed so often that the colour had faded.

Scant mention is made to City's change strip at this time being 'plum' coloured, although I have been unable to trace the source. Perhaps this would explain why in more recent years the club has worn maroon as their change strip.

CONCERTS. During recent years City have been in the forefront in England of maximising the use of their ground outside of the normal football season. They have been following the American example of using sports stadiums as venues for rock concerts during the summer months.

Stars of the magnitude of Pink Floyd, Jean Michel Jarre and, most recently, Rod Stewart, have all appeared at Maine

Road, and whilst obviously providing considerable income for the club, one can't help but have some sympathy for the beleaguered eardrums of the Moss Side residents.

CONNOR, DAVID, born Manchester, 27 October 1945. Short and stockily built, Wythenshawe-born David Connor was originally a left-winger in the City Youth team of 1963/64, but became something of a utility player once he had broken into the senior side a year later.

Connor, wearing the number eleven shirt, made his debut in a 2–1 defeat at Charlton on 22 August 1964. He was used in a variety of positions, including both full-backs, but really achieved his reputation when asked by Joe Mercer and Malcolm Allison to perform a man-marking role on the opposition's most dangerous player in crucial matches.

Many a rival team's key performer found himself frustrated by the close attentions of Connor, and perhaps his greatest performance came in the 1969 FA Cup semi-final when he completely stifled Everton's England star, Alan Ball.

David Connor's versatility however, was possibly his own worst enemy. He could never find himself a settled place and did not play in any of City's trophy-winning sides of that era, and, indeed, played in only ten full matches in the 1967/68 Championship season.

Finally after only 152 (+3) league and cup appearances for City in more than nine years, Connor moved to Preston North End on 21 January 1972 for a fee of £38,890, in a double deal with Neil Young. He spent three seasons at Deepdale before returning to Maine Road on a free transfer in March 1974 to play in the reserve side. Connor finished his playing career at non-league Macclesfield Town.

COOKSON, SAMMY, born Manchester, 22 November 1896. A miner who joined City in October 1918 from Macclesfield Town, Sammy Cookson was to form a long standing full-back partnership with Eli Fletcher which was to serve the club magnificently for many years.

Often described as 'the best uncapped full-back of his generation', Cookson was a short, powerfully built man, whose muscular appearance bore witness to his mining roots. It gave him a low centre of gravity which made it extremely difficult for wingers to get the better of him.

Despite 306 appearances for the club, Cookson's only reward was an FA Cup runners-up medal in 1926, scant reward for such a loyal servant. On 28 September 1928, he left to join Bradford, and later played for Barnsley, where, to his immense delight, he was to win a Third Division North Championship medal at the age of 38.

CORRIGAN, JOE, born Manchester, 18 November 1948. This giant of a goalkeeper had something of a topsy-turvy beginning to his career at Maine Road. Signed from amateur side Sale on 24 September 1966, Corrigan's debut in the first team came on 11 October 1967, in a 1–1 draw with Blackpool in the League Cup. Standing in for the injured Harry Dowd and the cup-tied Ken Mulhearn, Corrigan had the terrible misfortune to let Blackpool's goal go between his legs.

Despite this dreadful start, and being third choice keeper, he was determined to be successful. Armed already with a big heart, tremendous effort and commitment, Corrigan worked at his game with Malcolm Allison, and would eventually become one of the top three goalkeepers in the country.

Once established, despite the arrival of £100,000 Keith MacRae and being transfer-listed by Ron Saunders, Corrigan, a great favourite with the crowd, was to play 16 seasons at Maine Road. In total he played 592 games, placing him second behind Alan Oakes in City's all time appearances table. Corrigan won two League Cup winners' medals, a European Cup Winners' Cup medal and nine England caps, a figure which would undoubtedly have been higher but for the presence of Peter Shilton and Ray Clemence.

On 25 March 1983, he left Maine Road for a spell with Seattle Sounders in the NASL, before returning to England with Brighton and Hove Albion six months later.

COTON, TONY, born Tamworth, 19 May 1961. One of the most widely heard sayings amongst Manchester City supporters is 'We've always had good goalkeepers.' Following on in the legendary tradition of Frank Swift, Bert Trautmann and Joe Corrigan is today's first choice, Tony Coton.

Howard Kendall signed Coton from Watford on 12 July 1990, for a fee of £1 million. He had a difficult settling in period at Maine Road, with a certain section of the crowd angered by the replacement of the popular Andy Dibble. During this time, Coton considered leaving Maine Road, but following discussions with several backroom staff, fortunately decided to stay on.

By the end of the 1991/92 season, such was Coton's obvious ability, he had managed not only to win the support of the fans, but also City's coveted Player of the Year trophy.

A brave and commanding goalkeeper, often heard bellowing orders to his defence, Coton began his career at Birmingham City, where he saved a penalty after only 54 seconds of his debut.

At the time of writing, injuries, and selection errors, have prevented 'England's Number One' from playing in that position. A situation which hopefully will be remedied in the near future.

COWAN, SAM, born Chesterfield, 10 May 1901. Manager David Ashworth acquired the services of centre-half Sam Cowan from Doncaster Rovers on 12 December 1924. That position had been unsettled since the departure of the gentlemanly Max Woosnam, and once Cowan had established himself in the side, (having made his debut in a 2–2 draw against Birmingham City at Maine Road on 20 December), that particular problem didn't arise again for the next eleven seasons.

During that time, Cowan played 407 times for the Blues, scoring 24 goals.

His main asset of stopping the opposition disguised somewhat his likeness to attack on occasion, and in one game for Doncaster, he actually scored a hat-trick of headers.

Cowan also played in three FA Cup finals, winning only once, but that success in 1934 must have been extra special.

The previous year, following a 3–0 Wembley defeat by Everton, losing captain Cowan was consoled by King George V; 'You played well'. Despite tears in his eyes, Cowan replied, 'Thank you sir, but we'll be back next year and win it'.

Cowan left Maine Road as a player on 17 October 1935 to join Bradford City and then moved on to Brighton & HA as trainer. He settled on the south coast, eventually setting up a physiotherapist practice in Hove.

In November 1946, City approached Cowan with a view to his becoming team manager, replacing Wilf Wild who had been appointed secretary. That first season 1946/47 saw City win the Second Division title, but with Cowan still living in Hove, the situation was obviously far from ideal. Cowan's decision to concentrate full time on his physiotherapy practice in July 1947 meant he and City parted again. A City supporter right up to the end, Sam Cowan died whilst refereeing a charity match in October 1964.

CROSSAN, JOHNNY, born Derry, Northern Ireland, 29 November 1938. In January 1959, a lifetime ban was imposed on Johnny Crossan, following alleged irregularities over a proposed move to Bristol City. It meant that the little Irishman, who had started his career with Derry City and then Coleraine, was forced to look to Europe if he wished to continue playing.

Crossan signed for Dutch side Sparta Rotterdam, before moving on to Standard Liege of Belgium, for whom he played in the European Cup. This experience helped develop his already considerable talents, and when the ban was lifted in October 1962, he was a regular Irish international valued at £28,000 by Liege when Sunderland brought him back to English football.

On 22 January 1965, City paid Sunderland £40,000 for his services, and Crossan became an instant crowd favourite as his twinkle-toed midfield skills and inspiring captaincy, coupled with the expertise of Mercer and Allison, led the Blues back to the First Division at the end of the 1965/66 season.

Johnny Crossan played regularly for City on their return to the top flight, but, on 23 August 1967, he found himself surplus to requirements, and moved to Middlesbrough for a fee of £34,500. His career at Maine Road consisted of 110 league and cup games, with 28 goals.

CUPS. Taking all major cup competitions into account, City have lifted the silverware on eight occasions. They are:

FA CUP

23 April 1904	at Crystal Palace 1–0 v Bolton (Meredith) att. 61,374
28 April 1934	at Wembley 2–1 v Portsmouth (Tilson 2) att. 93,258
5 May 1956	at Wembley 3–1 v Birmingham (Johnstone, Hayes, Dyson) att. 100,000
26 April 1969	at Wembley 1–0 v Leicester (Young) att. 100,000

FOOTBALL LEAGUE CUP

7 March 1970	at Wembley 2–1 v WBA (Pardoe, Doyle) att. 97,963
28 Feb. 1976	at Wembley 2–1 v Newcastle (Barnes, Tueart) att. 100,000

EUROPEAN CUP WINNERS' CUP

29 April 1970	at The Prater Stadium, Vienna 2–1 v Gornik Zabzre (Young, Lee pen) att. 10,000

FA YOUTH CUP

1st leg	24 April 1986 v Manchester United at Old Trafford 1–1 (Lake) att. 7,602
2nd leg	29 April 1986 v Manchester United at Maine Road 2–0 (Moulden, Boyd) att. 18,164 City winning 3–1 on aggregate

CURLE, KEITH, born Bristol, 14 November 1963. The current City captain, Keith Curle's signing smashed the club's previous record when player/manager Peter Reid paid £2.5 million for him on 6 August 1991. Wimbledon were the recipients of this fee, which made Curle the most expensive defender in British football. He had spells at both his hometown clubs, as well as Torquay United and Reading, before arriving at Wimbledon in October 1988 as a replacement for Brian Gayle, who had moved to Maine Road.

His debut for City came in the opening game of the 1991/92 season, a 1–0 victory at Coventry. His tremendous pace and ability to read the game have made him a firm favourite with the Maine Road faithful, and despite being a central defender, he is also the regular penalty taker.

Admired by many of his contemporaries, it is somewhat surprising that at present, he has won only three international caps.

Keith Curle (Empics Ltd)

D

DALE, BILL, born Manchester, 17 February 1905. Bill Dale had played in only 64 league games in six years for Manchester United before a double move, along with Jack Rowley, to Maine Road on 23 December 1931.

This move not only gave him regular first team football, but also considerably more success. As City's first choice left-back over the next seven seasons, Dale made 269 league and cup appearances, won FA Cup winners' and runners'-up medals, and a First Division Championship medal in 1937.

He was considered unlucky at the time not to play for England, the left-back position being held then by the consistent Eddie Hapgood of Arsenal.

On 21 June 1938, Dale left Maine Road for Ipswich Town, staying in East Anglia during the war where he guested for Norwich City. He died in Manchester in June 1987.

DALEY, STEVE, born Barnsley, 15 April 1953. The signing of Steve Daley from Wolves on 5 September 1979 for an astonishing £1,437,500 set tongues wagging up and down the country, let alone in Manchester. The enormous price-tag placed on the midfielder's shoulders was perhaps the real reason why he was not a great success at Maine Road.

Daley was certainly experienced enough, having played nearly 250 games for Wolves, but his performances in a City shirt were to lead to several public disagreements between chairman Peter Swales and manager Malcolm Allison, as to just who had authorised the expense.

His debut came on 8 September 1979, in a game which saw City lose 1–0 to Southampton at Maine Road. He had made just 53 (+1) appearances for City, scoring four times, when new manager John Bond sold him to American side Seattle Sounders on 24 February 1981.

Daley played three seasons in Seattle before being tempted back to English football by Burnley in November 1983.

DAVIES, WYN, born Caernarvon, 20 March 1942. 'Wyn the Leap' joined City from Newcastle United on 2 August 1971 for a fee of £52,500.

One of the best headers of a ball in the Football League, the Welsh international centre-forward provided a perfect foil for Francis Lee, enabling Lee to score a remarkable 33 goals during that 1971/72 season. Davies missed only two league games in his first year at Maine Road, scoring eight times, as the Blues finished fourth in the First Division.

The opening game of the 1972/73 season saw Davies sent off at Anfield, and he played only two further games for City before a surprise move to Old Trafford on 14 September. The fee being £60,000.

Having played for Wrexham and Bolton prior to Newcastle, Davies left Manchester United in June 1973, later playing for Blackpool, Crystal Palace, Stockport County and Crewe.

DEFEAT – HEAVIEST
City's heaviest defeats in the three major domestic competitions are:

LEAGUE   1–9 v Everton (a) Division One
                3 September 1906
FA CUP   0–6 v Preston NE (a) Round One
                1 January 1897
LEAGUE CUP 0–6 v Birmingham C. (a) Round Five
                11 December 1962

DERBIES. The first Manchester 'derby' to take place in the Football League was at City's Hyde Road ground on 3 November 1894. The Division Two clash was Billy Meredith's first home game for City, and although he managed to score twice, Newton Heath, (as United were then called), ran out 5–2 victors.

City's first derby victory came on 7 December 1895, when Meredith's name again appeared on the score sheet, as the Blues won 2–1. The first actual Manchester City v Manchester United game was on Christmas Day 1902, when a crowd of nearly 40,000 packed into United's ground in Clayton to witness a 1–1 draw.

Some memorable City victories in league derbies are:

4–1 (home) 22 October 1921   – The last derby at Hyde Road.

6–1 (away) 23 January 1926   – Despite scoring more goals than in any other derby, City were still relegated at the end of the season.

3–1 (away) 7 February 1931   – Matt Busby's one and only Blue derby and United were relegated.

5–0 (away) 12 February 1955   – City's third victory of the season over United.

3–2 (away) 15 September 1962   – Two goals up after 25 minutes, Denis Law scores twice for United, only to see Alex Harley grab a last-minute winner.

3–1 (away) 27 March 1968   – City on their way to the Division One title.

4–0 (home) 15 November 1969   – Newspapers report on the most one-sided derby of all time.

4–1 (away) 12 December 1970   – Hat-trick for Francis Lee.

| 1–0 (away) 27 April 1974 | – Denis Law's 84th-minute backheel relegates United. |
| 5–1 (home) 23 September 1989 | – Undoubtedly the greatest derby day in living memory. |

City's overall league record, up to the end of the 1994/95 season is:

P	W	D	L	F	A
122	32	44	46	164	178

The clubs have met only five times in the FA Cup. The first game was a resounding 5–1 victory for Newton Heath over Ardwick on 3 October 1891. The Reds were to triumph again (this time 1–0), when the two teams last met, at Old Trafford, on 10 January 1987.

City's record is:

P	W	D	L	F	A
5	2	0	3	6	9

The League Cup has thrown up even fewer meetings, just four in fact, and one of these was over two legs. This was the semi-final of the 1969/70 tournament, when the Blues won 2–1 at Maine Road on 3 December, and managed a 2–2 draw at Old Trafford fourteen days later.

On 9 October 1974, a Gerry Daly penalty won the game for United in the fourth-round tie.

The following season saw the sides drawn together again, this time at Maine Road on 12 November, when a crowd of over 50,000 saw a convincing 4–0 Blues victory. This triumph was marred however by the terrible injury sustained by Colin Bell following a collision with Martin Buchan.

City's record is:

P	W	D	L	F	A
4	2	1	1	8	4

DEYNA, KAZIMIERZ, born Starogard Gdansk, Poland, 23 October 1947. A skilful, attacking right-sided midfield player, 'Kazzy' Deyna arrived at Maine Road on 9 November 1978. A player of great experience, Deyna had played nearly 500 times for Polish army side Legia Warsaw, scored nearly 200 goals, and captained Poland in two World Cups.

Manager Tony Book had decided overseas influence was required at Maine Road, obviously based on the popularity and success of Ardiles and Villa at Tottenham, and Deyna's first game for City was the 2–1 home defeat by Ipswich Town on 25 November.

He was to make just 38 (+5) appearances for City, scoring 13 times, before John Bond sold him to San Diego Sockers of the NASL on 28 January 1981.

After his retirement from the game in 1988, Deyna stayed on in the United States to coach youngsters. Tragically, he was killed in a road accident in California in September 1989.

DIBBLE, ANDY, born Cwmbran, 8 May 1965. But for the presence of Everton's Neville Southall, Andy Dibble would certainly be Wales' automatic first-choice goalkeeper.

Signed by Cardiff City on apprentice forms, Dibble made his first team debut on his 17th birthday. Two years later, he had moved on to Luton Town, where he will best be remembered for saving a penalty at Wembley, when Luton beat Arsenal in the 1988 Littlewoods' Cup Final.

To broaden his experience, Dibble spent periods on loan at Sunderland and Huddersfield before Mel Machin and a tribunal fee of £240,000 brought him to Maine Road on 8 June 1988. He was the Blues' first-choice keeper for the following two seasons, but the arrival of the £1 million Tony Coton in the summer of 1990 forced Dibble into the reserve side.

Further loan spells at Aberdeen, Middlesbrough, Bolton and WBA put Dibble's Maine Road career in doubt, but injuries to Coton in the last two seasons gave him extended runs in the first team.

DOBING, PETER, born Manchester, 1 December 1938. After scoring 88 goals in 179 appearances for Blackburn Rovers, inside-forward Peter Dobing signed for City on 17 July 1961. His transfer fee had been financed by the sale of Denis Law to Torino, and he made his debut in the opening game of the 1961/62 season, a 3–1 home win against Leicester. Dobing missed only one league game that season, scoring 22 times, including three hat-tricks, as City finished 12th in Division One. A further 41 league games followed the next season, but Dobing could only find the net nine times. Newly signed Scot Alex Harley topped the list that season with 23. Harley's presence, inconsistent team formations, and ultimately relegation to the Second Division, forced Dobing to finally seek a transfer. On 15 August 1963, he signed for Stoke City, where he played more than 300 games, and won a League Cup winners' medal.

DOHERTY, PETER, born Magherafelt, Northern Ireland, 5 June 1913. Quite simply, one of the greatest British footballers of all time.

Peter Doherty's supreme talents never earned him the international recognition he deserved because he was Irish rather than English. City paid a then club record fee of £10,000 to Blackpool for his services on 19 February 1936, three years after the Seasiders had recruited him from his native Northern Ireland. He had been a star already at home, firstly with Coleraine and then Glentoran, and within a short space of time, the flame-haired Doherty had achieved superstar status with the adoring City public.

His artistry and boundless energy made him the outstanding all-round footballer of his time. He could tackle like a full-back, head like a centre-half, and possessed a deadly touch in front of goal.

Doherty's 30 goals were the inspiration behind the League Championship success of 1936/37, but World War Two prematurely ended his City career after only 130 league and cup appearances and 79 goals.

Although still registered as a player at Maine Road throughout the war (as well as being in the RAF), he was allowed to join Derby County on 6 December 1945, and helped them win the FA Cup that same season.

Doherty later moved into league and international management, and led Northern Ireland to the quarter-finals of the 1958 World Cup. Capped 16 times for his country, Peter Doherty died in Poulton-le-Fylde in April 1990, aged 76.

DONACHIE, WILLIE, born Glasgow, 5 October 1951. More than 25 years after signing for City, Willie Donachie is still involved with a Premier League side. He is currently number two to another former City star, Joe Royle, at Goodison Park, a position he has held since November 1994. This is by no means a new partnership, however, as they began a successful managerial career together back in July 1984, when they began to transform Oldham Athletic.

It was as a midfielder that Donachie signed for City on 12 December 1968. Coming from Glasgow Amateurs, City turned him into a full-back, and he made his senior appearance against Nottingham Forest on 7 February 1970, when, as a substitute, he replaced the injured Tony Book.

Donachie would eventually become City's regular number three, a shirt he would wear with distinction for nearly eight seasons, before he moved to American side Portland Timbers on 19 March 1980. 421 (+5) appearances place Donachie tenth in the overall table at Maine Road, although he could only manage two goals. Only Asa Hartford, with 36, has won more Scottish caps as a City player. Donachie is just one behind, on 35.

DOWD, HARRY, born Manchester, 4 July 1938. A plumber by trade, Harry Dowd did not turn professional until he was 22 years old, and then the young goalkeeper made a nightmare start to his career at Maine Road. Signed from ICI Blackley on 10 January 1958, Dowd stood in for the injured Bert Trautmann and conceded ten goals in his first two games. The Blues lost 4–1 at Blackburn on 9 December 1961, and then 6–3 at Burnley on 13 January the following year. It says much for his temperament and resolve that he was able to bounce back for the 1962/63 season and eventually replace the legendary German. Unfortunaely for Dowd, City were relegated that term, and he became the number one choice in a City side that would spend the next three years in the Second Division.

Despite being on the short side for a goalkeeper, Dowd was to prove a major force for the Blues in the mid to late 60s, helping them to win both the Second Division Championship and the FA Cup. Injury cost him his place in the 1968 Championship side, when Ken Mulhearn took over in goal.

Unusually Harry Dowd's name is in the record books as a goalscorer. On 8 February 1964, in a home game against Bury, Dowd was led off the field with a broken finger after making a diving save at an opponent's feet. He returned to the action later with his arm in a sling, and for the last 36 minutes of the game played up front purely as nuisance value. With time running out and City a goal down, the injured goalkeeper proved an unlikely hero when he slid in an equaliser after a shot from Derek Kevan had bounced down off the bar.

On 1 December 1970, after 219 league and cup appearances and that one special goal, Harry Dowd left City for Oldham Athletic, where he added to his reputation by helping Latics rise from the Fourth to the Second Division.

DOYLE, MIKE, born Stockport, 25 November 1946. It was often said that self-confessed United hater Mike Doyle had 'blue blood running through his veins', and it is true that there were fewer players more committed to the City cause during his long career at Maine Road.

The son of a policeman, the former Stockport Boys player signed for City straight from school on 11 May 1962, and featured as a right-back in the young Blues' team which reached the FA Youth Cup semi-final in 1963/64.

After turning professional in May 1964, Doyle made his senior debut in a Second Division game at Cardiff on 12 March 1965, as a wing-half, where his determination and aggression were better suited. Although not liking the position, Doyle was also used up front in the number nine shirt, but he eventually settled into midfield where his influence helped City to the Second Division title in 1965/66, and then the First Division Championship two years later.

Doyle was a key figure at Maine Road over the next ten seasons, gaining FA Cup and European Cup Winners' Cup medals, and playing in three League Cup finals. City won two of these, Doyle himself scoring in the 1970 triumph over WBA, and lifting the trophy as captain six years later after Dennis Tueart's bicycle-kick had beaten Newcastle United.

By 1976, Doyle had moved into the back four, where he won five full England caps to add to his Under-23 and Football League honours. On 5 June 1978, Mike Doyle was transferred to Stoke City for £50,000. His total of 551 (+7) first team appearances placing him third in the all time list of great Maine Road servants.

DYSON, JACKIE, born Oldham, 8 July 1934. Signed from non-league Nelson on 12 June 1952, centre-forward Jackie Dyson also played 150 first-class cricket matches for Lancashire. It was during the summer of 1956, following City's Wembley triumph over Birmingham (when Dyson scored), that he became the joint owner of a never before, or since, equalled cricketing record.

He and the other opener Alan Wharton were the only two batsmen used in either innings, as Lancashire beat Leicestershire by ten wickets at Old Trafford.

Despite being at Maine Road for ten years, Dyson's appearances were limited to just 71, scoring 29 goals in the process. During his playing career, Dyson suffered a broken leg twice. The irony being that it was team-mate Bill Leivers who broke his leg the first time in a pre-season public practice match at Maine Road.

Dyson was dismissed by Lancashire in 1960 after a serious breach of discipline, and on 30 March 1961, he left City to join Stirling Albion.

E

EDGHILL, RICHARD, born Oldham, 23 September 1974. A fast and skilful full-back, equally at home in the centre of defence, Richard Edghill joined City as a schoolboy in November 1988, turning professional in July 1992. These qualities, when linked with a good passing ability and calmness disguising his years, quickly established him as a regular in the reserve side. Following a good start to the Central League season of 1992/93, Edghill found himself called to Lilleshall in preparation for the World Youth Cup. Sadly, he was not chosen for the final party, but his continued fine performances with the reserves would eventually give him a chance of first team football. This opportunity came in a 1–0 defeat at Wimbledon on 20 September 1993, just three days before his 19th birthday. A young man with a very bright future had arrived at Maine Road.

EIRE – FIRST CITY PLAYER. The first City player to represent the Republic of Ireland was Dublin-born Leo Dunne.

Dunne played only three games for City, two in 1933/34 and one the following season, but managed to play twice for Eire during the same period. These games were both in 1935, against Switzerland and Germany.

ENGLAND – FIRST CITY PLAYER. At the time of writing, 33 Manchester City players have represented England at full international level. The first of these was Herbert 'The Mighty Atom' Burgess, back in 1904 against Wales.

Like City's first Eire representative Dunne, 31 years later, Burgess too was a left-back, who was banned from playing for City in 1906 after the alleged bribes scandal.

Burgess won all of his four caps whilst at Hyde Road, before moving to Manchester United, and later he coached in Europe.

EUROPEAN CUP. Following their First Division success in 1967/68, City were in the European Cup for the first time.

Malcolm Allison made his now infamous 'We will terrify Europe' comment, and, as all Blues followers now know, City fell at the first hurdle.

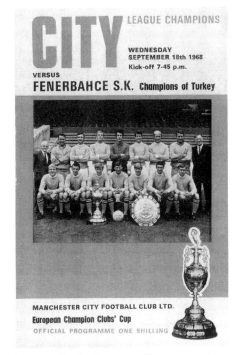

To date, City's one and only European Cup game at home – a goalless draw with Turkish champions Fenerbahçe

Turkish champions Fenerbahçe visited Maine Road for the first round, first leg game on 18 September 1968. A crowd of 38,787 saw City struggle, and a goalless draw meant that all the hard work had to be done in the away leg.

At half-time in the second leg, played on 2 October, the prospects for the Blues looked good. A goal by winger Tony Coleman had given City the lead, but by the end of the game, 45,000 delirious Turks had seen Fenerbahçe score twice in reply to win the game, and the tie, 2–1.

EUROPEAN CUP WINNERS' CUP. City took the lessons learnt the previous season into the 1969/70 European Cup Winners' Cup. Determined not to repeat the Fenerbahçe tragedy, City's eventual success in this competition, coupled with a League Cup triumph over WBA, meant the Blues became the first side ever to win both a domestic and European trophy in the same season.

The European Cup Winners' Cup games that year were:

Round One	1st leg	17 Sept 1969	3–3 v Atletico Bilbao	(a)
	2nd leg	1 Oct 1969	3–0 v Atletico Bilbao	(h)
Round Two	1st leg	12 Nov 1969	3–0 v SK Lierse	(a)
	2nd leg	26 Nov 1969	5–0 v SK Lierse	(h)
Round Three	1st leg	4 March 1970	0–0 v Academica Coimbra	(a)
	2nd leg	18 March 1970	1–0 v Academica Coimbra	(h)
Semi-Final	1st leg	1 April 1970	0–1 v FC Schalke 04	(a)
	2nd leg	15 April 1970	5–1 v FC Schalke 04	(h)
Final		29 April 1970	2–1 v Gornik Zabrze	
			The Prater Stadium, Vienna	

The 22 goals that season came from: Francis Lee 6

Colin Bell 5

Neil Young 4

and one each from Tommy Booth

Ian Bowyer

Alan Oakes

Mike Summerbee

Tony Towers

Mike Doyle

Opp. own goal

City's defence of the trophy began on 16 September 1970.

The results that season were:

Round One	1st leg	16 Sep 1970	1–0 v Linfield	(h)
	2nd leg	30 Sep 1970	1–2 v Linfield	(a)
	City went through on away goals.			
Round Two	1st leg	21 Oct 1970	1–0 v Honved	(a)
	2nd leg	4 Nov 1970	2–0 v Honved	(h)
Round Three	1st leg	10 March 1971	0–2 v Gornik Zabrze	(a)
	2nd leg	24 March 1971	2–0 v Gornik Zabrze	(h)
	Replay	31 March 1971	3–1 v Gornik Zabrze	
	In Copenhagen			
Semi Final	1st leg	14 April 1971	0–1 v Chelsea	(h)
	2nd leg	28 April 1971	0–1 v Chelsea	(a)

But for a horrendous list of injuries towards the end of that campaign, City were quietly confident that they would retain the trophy.

The ten goals that season were scored by: Francis Lee 4
Colin Bell 2
and one each from Ian Mellor
Mike Doyle
Tommy Booth
Neil Young

The club's overall record in the European Cup Winners' Cup is:

P	W	D	L	F	A
18	11	2	5	32	13

EWING, DAVE, born Perth, 10 May 1929. 'All stop at Dave's', was a popular saying among City supporters of the 1950s in tribute to the no-nonsense, 'they shall not pass', attitude of their centre-half.

A craggy, powerful defender of the old school, Dave Ewing joined City from Luncarty Juniors on 10 June 1949. He had to wait until 3 January 1953 for a memorable first team debut, in the Manchester derby at Old Trafford, when he earned great praise for an uncompromising display in a 1–1 draw.

It was the first of many such performances over the next few years, as he established a reputation for being one of the toughest centre-halves in the game. His booming voice also became a thing of Maine Road legend as he constantly harangued his team-mates and exhorted them to greater efforts.

Ewing was the defensive cornerstone of a City side which reached successive FA Cup finals, and he earned a winners' medal in the 1956 victory over Birmingham City.

After 302 league and cup appearances for City, he joined Crewe on 7 July 1962, but returned to Maine Road in a coaching capacity within a couple of years. Ewing was later employed by Sheffield Wednesday, Bradford City, Crystal Palace and Hibernian.

F

FA CUP – FIRST APPEARANCE. 20 July 1871 saw the birth of the FA Cup. Only 15 clubs entered that year, and the 18-inch silver trophy, costing £20 and christened 'The Little Tin Idol', was won by The Wanderers, who beat The Royal Engineers 1–0 at Kennington Oval on 16 March 1872.

It was not until 4 October 1890, that Ardwick played their first game in the FA Cup. This was a qualifying round one tie against Liverpool Stanley at Hyde Road. Ardwick destroyed their visitors 12–0, and this is still the Blues' record FA Cup victory.

Although Manchester City came into being at the beginning of the 1894/95 season, they did not compete in the FA Cup that term. The following season, City were drawn against Oswaldtwistle Rovers in the qualifying round, but withdrew from the competition shortly before the October tie.

Their first appearance in the competition actually took place on 1 January 1897. City played away at Preston North End in the first round, and were resoundingly beaten 6–0. This game also provides a club record. It is City's highest FA cup defeat of all time.

FA CUP FINALS. Up to the end of the 1994/95 season, City have appeared in eight FA Cup finals. They have had mixed fortunes in these games, having both won, and lost, four times.

The victories occurred in:

1904 23 April 1–0 v Bolton Wanderers at The Crystal Palace.

City – Hillman, McMahon, Burgess, Frost, Hynds, Ashworth, Meredith, Livingstone, Gillespie, Turnbull, Booth. A crowd of 61,374 sees Billy Meredith's goal win the Cup for City.

1934 28 April 2–1 v Portsmouth at Wembley

City – Swift, Barnett, Dale, Busby, Cowan, Bray, Toseland, Marshall, Tilson, Herd, Brook. Fred Tilson scores twice in front of a crowd of 93,258.

The victorious 1934 FA Cup final side as depicted in the matchday programme

1956 5 May 3–1 v Birmingham City at Wembley
      City – Trautmann, Leivers, Little, Barnes, Ewing,
          Paul, Johnstone, Hayes, Revie, Dyson,
          Clarke.
          A capacity crowd of 100,000 watch the Blues'
          triumph, thanks to goals from Johnstone,
          Hayes and Dyson.
1969 26 April 1–0 v Leicester City at Wembley
      City – Dowd, Book, Pardoe, Doyle, Booth, Oakes,
          Summerbee, Bell, Lee, Young, Coleman.
          Neil Young's 23rd-minute goal proves
          enough to clinch victory. Leicester suffer the
          unenviable misfortune of Cup runners-up and
          relegation to the Second Division. The last
          time this occurred was 1926. The team then
          was Manchester City.

*Bert Trautman and the injured Jimmy Meadows console each other after
the 1955 FA Cup final. The following year things would be different
(News Team International)*

City suffered defeats in:

1926 24 April 0–1 v Bolton Wanderers at Wembley.
1933 29 April 0–3 at Everton at Wembley.
1955 7 May   1–3 v Newcastle United at Wembley.
               Bobby Johnstone's strike not enough for
               City.
1981 14 May 2–3 v Tottenham Hotspur at Wembley.
               Steve MacKenzie's volley and a penalty
               from Kevin Reeves fail to give City victory
               in this replay.
               Five days earlier, a goal at both ends by
               Tommy Hutchison made the result 1–1.

FA CUP SEMI-FINALS. As already mentioned, City have appeared in eight FA Cup finals. In addition to those eight, the Blues have taken part in two other, unsuccessful, semi-finals.

The following is a list of all ten semi-finals:

1904 19 March   3–1 v Sheffield Wednesday at Goodison
                 Park
1924 29 March   0–2 v Newcastle United at St. Andrews
1926 27 March   3–0 v Manchester United at Bramall Lane
1932 12 March   0–1 v Arsenal at Villa Park
1933 18 March   3–2 v Derby County at Leeds Road
1934 17 March   6–1 v Aston Villa at Leeds Road
1955 26 March   1–0 v Sunderland at Villa Park
1956 17 March   1–0 v Tottenham Hotspur at Villa Park
1969 22 March   1–0 v Everton at Villa Park
1981 11 April   1–0 v Ipswich Town at Villa Park

FAGAN, FIONAN, 'PADDY', born Dublin, 7 June 1930. The son of an Irish international, 'Paddy' Fagan was a tricky two-footed winger who followed his father into the Republic side soon after joining City from Hull City on Christmas Eve 1953, his debut coming two days later in a 2–1 home win against Sheffield United. He became a regular over the next five seasons, and his ability to operate on both flanks proved a useful asset in a Blues' side that reached successive FA Cup finals in 1955 and 1956. Fagan played in the first of these finals, a 3–1 defeat by Newcastle

United, but missed out the following year when City were successful against Birmingham City.

After 164 first team appearances and 35 goals for City, Fagan left Maine Road for Derby County on 15 March 1960, for £8,000.

FAGAN, JOE, born Liverpool, 12 March 1921. Like Matt Busby, Joe Fagan will be remembered for his managerial successes with another club, rather than for his playing days with City. Centre-half Fagan signed for the Blues from Earlstown Bohemians on 8 October 1938. World War Two delayed his league debut until 1 January 1947, in a game which saw City beat Fulham 4–0 at Maine Road. (He had played four games the previous season in the wartime Football League North).

Fagan played 20 times during his first season, in which City won the Second Division Championship, and he missed only three league games in the next three seasons.

After five games of the 1950/51 season, Fagan left Maine Road for non-league Nelson, but later returned to league football with Bradford Park Avenue. In 1953 he became trainer at Rochdale, before finally moving to Anfield, where he would eventually win three trophies in his first year as manager.

During his time with City, Fagan scored twice in 158 league and cup appearances.

FANZINES. Like most other clubs nowadays, City are no different when it comes to fanzines. These magazines have no official connection with the club, and the thoughts expressed within the pages are often critical, but on the whole very funny. Current City fanzines are *King of the Kippax* (produced by Dave 'Supporter on the Board' Wallace), *Electric Blue* and *The Charming Fan. Blueprint,* responsible for, and supportive of, the inflatable bananas, makes only an occasional appearance now, while it appears that *Main Stand View* and *Blue Murder* have disappeared for good.

FLETCHER, ELI, born Tunstall, 15 December 1887. The other half of City's formidable full-back pairing of the era,

Eli Fletcher was, like his long-time partner Sammy Cookson, a former miner, considered by many to be desperately unlucky not to become a regular for England.

Fletcher joined City on 18 May 1911 from Crewe Alexandra, for whom he had starred in a giant killing FA Cup win at First Division Bristol City. So impressed were the West Country club with Fletcher that they too tried to sign him, but he opted for Manchester for a fee of £300.

He became captain and one of City's longest serving players, clocking up 326 league and cup appearances, despite sustaining a serious knee injury against Birmingham City in 1922 that threatened his career. Fletcher's determination shone through, and he actually turned out in goal for the reserve side whilst battling his way back to full fitness. This serious injury, which would have finished many lesser players, kept him out of first team action for just nine months. Despite his success on the field, his personal life was dogged by tragedy, and he lost two daughters and his only son in the space of three years.

With 138 wartime appearances added to his total, Eli Fletcher can be seen as one of City's most loyal servants. His loyalty was rewarded with a testimonial in 1922, when he was allowed to keep the receipts of a home game against Sheffield United.

On 2 June 1926, Eli Fletcher left Maine Road to become player/manager with Watford.

FLITCROFT, GARRY, born Bolton, 6 November 1972. Such is the talent of this England Under-21 international midfielder, that City were just one of four clubs the schoolboy Flitcroft could have signed for.

He joined City in July 1989 as a trainee, eventually becoming a paid player two summers later. Since his first team debut against Oldham Athletic on 29 August 1992, Flitcroft's abilities have also been displayed at full-back and in the centre of defence.

A strong and whole-hearted player, Flitcroft gained senior experience during a two-month loan period at Bury at the end of his debut season. The summer of 1993 brought the first of his Under-21 honours, after he had established himself as a regular in the Blues' first team at the beginning of the 1992/93 season. His impact on the field during that season enabled him to win City's Player of the Year trophy nine months later.

The young man responsible for an outbreak of new look haircuts among the younger supporters, is tipped by many to have a great future in the game. No City fan would disagree with that statement.

FLOODLIGHTS. City's first game at Maine Road under floodlights took place on 14 October 1953. This was an arranged friendly against Scottish club Hearts, and the Blues wore 'special shirts with a shiny finish'. A crowd of 23,979 saw City triumph 6–3, thanks to a hat-trick from Sowden, two from Hart, and one from Broadis. A newspaper report described Hearts' three goals as 'a penalty, scrappy and lucky'. (Sentiments echoed countless times since!)

On 26 February 1889, Ardwick FC played Newton Heath under twenty 'Wells' floodlights at Belle Vue. Nearly 12,000 people witnessed a 3–2 victory for Newton Heath, as £140 was raised for the Hyde Colliery Explosion Fund.

FOOTBALL LEAGUE. Preston North End were the first winners of the Football League back in 1888/89.

It wasn't until the 1892/93 season that the name of Ardwick FC first appeared. That season the Hyde Road side finished fifth in the newly formed Division Two, 15 points behind the champions Small Heath, later to become Birmingham City.

Five seasons later, 1898/99, Manchester City won the first of their six Second Division Championships. The following season saw City establish themselves in the First Division by finishing in a creditable seventh position. However the next few years provided an early opportunity to witness the now legendary topsy-turvy performances of Manchester City.

1900/01   11th in Division One
1901/02   18th in Division One – relegated
1902/03   1st in Division Two – promoted

1903/04   2nd in Division One – and FA Cup winners
1904/05   3rd in Division One
1905/06   5th in Division One

City spent a further three seasons in Division One before being relegated again at the end of the 1908/09 season.

1909/10 proved once again a solitary Second Division season, as the Blues immediately won their third Championship, with exactly the same number of points as they had won their second, eight years earlier.

City's full record (to the end of the 1994/95 season) is:

HOME

	P	W	D	L	F	A
FA PREMIER LEAGUE (3 seasons)	63	21	25	17	91	75
DIVISION ONE (68 seasons)	1386	757	320	309	2623	1652
DIVISION TWO (21 seasons)	393	261	71	61	1061	445

AWAY

	P	W	D	L	F	A
FA PREMIER LEAGUE (3 seasons)	63	15	18	30	56	89
DIVISION ONE (68 seasons)	1386	304	357	725	1654	2580
DIVISION TWO (21 seasons)	393	141	102	150	591	637

TOTALS	P	W	D	L	F	A
HOME RECORD	1842	1039	416	387	3775	2172
AWAY RECORD	1842	460	476	905	2301	3306

TOTAL POINTS: FA PREMIER LEAGUE   151
                    DIVISION ONE   2905
                    DIVISION TWO   1060

                    Grand Total   4116

In 92 seasons, Ardwick and City's League successes have been:

Division One Champions	(2) – 1936/37, 1967/68
Runners-up	(3) – 1903/04, 1920/21, 1976/77
Division Two Champions	(6) – 1898/99, 1902/03, 1909/10, 1927/28, 1946/47, 1965/66
Runners-up	(3) – 1895/96, 1950/51, 1988/89

FOOTBALL LEAGUE CUP. The Football League Cup, known also by four other names, came into being in 1960. It was not accepted immediately by all clubs, and consequently several top flight teams did not compete.

City however, were one of the sides which did take part, and the Blues' first game in the new competition was against neighbours Stockport County on 18 October 1960.

A Maine Road crowd of 21,065 saw City run out 3–1 winners, with two goals from Denis Law, and one from Joe Hayes.

City's record (to the end of the 94/95 season) is:

P	W	D	L	F	A
142	73	31	38	257	165

During this time, the Blues have reached three Wembley finals, coming away with the cup on two occasions:

1970 7 March 2–1 v West Bromwich Albion
   City – Corrigan, Book, Mann, Doyle, Booth, Oakes, Heslop, Bell, Summerbee (Bowyer), Lee, Pardoe.
   A crowd of 97,963 see goals from Doyle and Pardoe clinch victory for City after going a goal behind. The match was played on one of Wembley's worst ever pitches, and came just three days after a third round ECWC tie in Portugal.

1974 3 March 1–2 v Wolverhampton Wanderers
   City – MacRae, Pardoe, Donachie, Doyle, Booth Towers, Summerbee, Bell, Lee, Law, Marsh.
   City's 50th League Cup game ends in defeat, as Wolves' keeper Gary Pierce stops everything except a solitary Colin Bell shot.

It is still hard to believe even 20 years later that one of City's greatest ever forward lines failed to secure victory.

1976 28 February 2–1 v Newcastle United
       City – Corrigan, Keegan, Donachie, Doyle, Watson, Oakes, Barnes, Booth, Royle, Hartford, Tueart.
       Perhaps the most spectacular League Cup goal ever, Dennis Tueart's bicycle-kick, clinches victory for the Blues following Peter Barnes' first-half strike.

FOOTBALLER OF THE YEAR Only three City players have won the prestigious Footballer of the Year trophy. They are: 1955 – Don Revie
1956 – Bert Trautmann
1969 – Tony Book (jointly with Derby's Dave Mackay)

FOREIGN PLAYERS WITH CITY

NAME	FROM	PLAYED
Baker, Gerry	United States	1960–1961
Bouvy, Nico J.J.	Holland	1914
Bowman, Walter	Canada	1892–1900
Deyna, Kazimierz	Poland	1978–1981
Gaudino, Maurizio	Germany	1995
Golac, Ivan	Yugoslavia	1983
Groenedijk, Alfons	Holland	1993–1994
Hareide, Aage	Norway	1981–1983
Hoekman, Danny	Holland	1991
Ingebrigtsen, Kaare	Norway	1993–1994
Karl, Steffen	Germany	1994
Kinkladze, Georgiou	Georgia	1995
Rösler, Uwe	Germany	1994–present
Stepanovic, Dragoslav	Yugoslavia	1979–1981
Trautmann, Bert	Germany	1949–1964
Viljoen, Colin	South Africa	1978–1980
Vonk, Michel	Holland	1992–present

FRANCIS, TREVOR, born Plymouth, 19 April 1954. Following eight seasons, and 118 league goals, with his first club Birmingham City, Trevor Francis became Britain's first £1 million footballer when he joined Nottingham Forest in February 1979.

On 3 September 1981, after European success with Forest, Francis signed for manager John Bond for a fee of £1.2 million. Two days later he made his debut for the Blues, scoring twice in a 3–1 away win at Stoke City.

The former teenage wonder of English soccer played 29 times and scored 14 goals during his one and only season at Maine Road. These figures would surely have been more but for two lengthy injuries sustained and, although a great favourite with the crowd, the management began to consider him a luxury.

On 30 July 1982, Italian giants Sampdoria lured Francis away from Maine Road for a fee of £800,000. He was to play for two other Italian sides, Genoa and Atalanta before returning to British football with Glasgow Rangers. In March 1988, Francis moved on again, this time to become player/manager with Queens Park Rangers, a position he later held with Sheffield Wednesday.

FRIZZELL, JIMMY, born Greenock, 16 February 1937. Jimmy Frizzell's playing career began with Scottish club Morton as a wing-half in 1957. In May 1960, he moved south to Oldham, where he began an association which was to last 22 years. As a player he scored 57 times in 309 league games for Latics, before taking over the manager's reigns in March 1970. Within 4 years of his appointment, he had guided the Boundary Park club from the Fourth to the Second Division.

In the summer of 1982, Frizzell was dismissed by Oldham, and spent the next twelve months out of the game before becoming Billy McNeill's assistant at Maine Road. When McNeill left in September 1986 for Aston Villa, Frizzell was promoted to manager, but survived only one season in charge as the Blues were relegated. At this point, Frizzell was moved to general manager, with Norwich coach Mel Machin coming in to take charge of team matters.

Still at Maine Road today, Jimmy Frizzell has held several different behind the scenes positions including stadium manager and is currently chief scout.

FULL MEMBERS' CUP. A trophy, which not unlike the League Cup, has had a series of different sponsors during its short life. Despite being known also as the Simod Cup and the Zenith Data Systems Cup, the tournament has always failed to grasp the imagination of the fans, who responded regularly with extremely poor attendances.

City's full record in the competition (all names) is:

P	W	D	L	F	A
17	8	1	8	37	29

These figures do not include City's 5–4 victory on penalties against Sunderland on 4 November 1985.

Top scorers for the Blues are; 3 Tony Adcock (hat-trick)
3 Gordon Davies (hat-trick)
3 Mark Lillis
3 David Phillips

On 23 March 1986, City lost 5–4 to Chelsea in the final at Wembley. A crowd of 68,000 saw that game, but an average gate (not including that Wembley final), is just 6,855.

FURNISS, LAWRENCE, Over the years, there have been many people who devoted large periods of their lives to Manchester City. Undoubtedly the first of these was Lawrence Furniss.

Originally a player with Gorton FC, his playing career was ended by a serious knee injury which forced him into football administration and in 1889 he became secretary of Ardwick FC.

His early work included the construction of a 1,000 spectator stand at Hyde Road, a princely first year end profit of £33, and he was credited by many for bringing Billy Meredith to Manchester City in October 1894.

Furniss's 'managerial' responsibilities had been given over to Joshua Parlby shortly before the name change, but such was his devotion to the cause, that he was involved with the club for a total of 46 years. He spent two periods on the board of directors, was club chairman from 1921 to 1928, and eventually became club president.

Lawrence Furniss, was probably the first 'true blue'.

FUTCHER, PAUL, born Chester, 25 September 1956. Central defender Paul Futcher joined the Blues from Luton Town on 1 June 1978. Manager Tony Book had paid a then club record fee of £350,000 for his services, but within two months of the start of the 1978/79 season, Futcher found it hard to maintain a regular first team spot.

Possibly a Steve Daley like 'price-tag' victim, Futcher played in just 24 league games that season, although he did win an England Under-21 cap.

On 31 July 1980, nearly two years after making his debut for City, Oldham boss Jimmy Frizzell signed Futcher for a fee of £150,000.

During his time at Maine Road, he played 44 (+2) league and cup games but never managed a senior goal. After leaving Boundary Park in January 1983, Futcher played for Derby County, Halifax Town and Grimsby Town, but will perhaps be best remembered for six years and 230 league games in Barnsley's colours.

FUTCHER, RON, born Chester, 25 September 1956. Twin brother of Paul, Ron had also played for Chester and Luton Town before his arrival at Maine Road. Technically he came to City from NASL side Minnesota Kicks on 22 August 1978, despite still being officially registered with Luton.

Futcher's third game for City saw him score a hat-trick in a 4–1 victory at Stamford Bridge. Although early signs looked good, he played only 10 (+7) league games during his one and only season at Maine Road, but he did score seven times.

On 14 April 1979, Futcher returned to Minnesota where he played over the next few summers. Again, like his brother Paul, Ron was a much travelled player. After leaving City, his career took him to Barnsley, Oldham, Bradford City, Port Vale, Burnley and Crewe.

G

GAUDINO, MAURIZIO, born Brule, Germany 12 December 1966. Despite the Italian-sounding name, Maurizio Gaudino is a cultured German midfielder, good enough to be a member of their national side in the 1994 World Cup finals.

Recommended to the Blues by the same man who had recommended Uwe Rösler, Gaudino was unsettled with his Bundesliga club Eintracht Frankfurt, and was delighted when City offered him a chance to play in the Premier League.

Signed initially on loan on 19 December 1994 for £210,000, Gaudino's first taste of English football came two days after his signing in a 2–0 Coca Cola Cup victory at Newcastle.

The holder of four full German caps found the English game much quicker, but would gradually improve his stamina, and his obvious skill shone through.

Prior to Frankfurt, Gaudino had played for TSG Rheingau, SV Waldhof Mannheim and VfB Stuttgart. Leeds United striker Tony Yeboah, a former team-mate at Frankfurt, has no doubt about Gaudino's ability to be a success in English football. He (along with many City fans) must have been shocked, therefore, when Gaudino decided to leave Maine Road in the summer of 1995 to return to Frankfurt.

GAYLE, BRIAN, born Kingston-on-Thames, 6 March 1965. Having played football in New Zealand, and basketball in his youth, Brian Gayle signed for Wimbledon in October 1984. On 9 June 1988, after 76 (+7) league appearances for the Dons, City, and £325,000, fought off the challenges of Arsenal and Crystal Palace for his signature.

Gayle made his City debut at Hull on 27 August that year, in a game the Blues lost 1–0. He played in all but five of City's 46 league games that season, one that saw promotion back to the top flight. The 1989/90 season continued the defensive partnership formed with Steve Redmond, and Gayle found himself captaining the side. However a managerial change and the arrival of Colin Hendry, both in November 1989, meant the writing was on the wall for Gayle.

On 17 January 1990, Gayle left Maine Road for Ipswich Town for a fee of £330,000, where he played for just over eighteen months before joining Sheffield United.

Gayle scored three times in 66 league and cup appearances for City.

GILLESPIE, BILLY, born Strathclyde. Billy Gillespie was a brawny Scot hugely popular at Hyde Road at the turn of the century, when his bustling centre-forward qualities brought him 132 goals from 230 league and cup appearances in an eight-year stay. These goals place him joint eighth overall for City.

He arrived at Hyde Road on 7 January 1897, making his debut two days later, when he scored in a 3–1 defeat at Darwen. Gillespie became the focal point for an attack which featured the likes of Meredith, Livingstone, Turnbull and Booth, and he helped City to two Second Division Championships, as well as an FA Cup triumph over Bolton in 1904.

He had always had something of a colourful, unorthodox reputation, but in the summer of 1905, his decision to quit football and emigrate to South Africa with his new bride came as a great shock to everyone in the game, not least his brother Matt, a player with rivals Newton Heath.

A year after he left England he was again surrounded in controversy, when he was fined and suspended by the FA for what were called 'transfer irregularities' in the infamous scandal that almost destroyed the club.

GOALKEEPERS. For some unknown reason, Manchester City, and high-quality goalkeepers have always been closely linked. Names such as Frank Swift, Bert Trautmann, Joe Corrigan and today's custodian, Tony Coton spring immediately to mind, but let us not forget others who have worn City's number one jersey with pride, and on occasion, hilarity:

J.F. Mitchell played 109 times for City in the early 1920s. Perhaps the only league goalkeeper ever to wear glasses whilst playing.

Harry Dowd played 219 times for the Blues in the 1960s, and managed to score a goal as an outfield player. Not a bad record for a plumber.

Jack Hillman played 124 games just after the turn of the century. Once accepted a bet to keep goal one handed in a charity match. His side won 1–0.

Charlie Williams was another eccentric who played 232 games between 1894 and 1902. Williams scored one of the first goals ever by a goalkeeper with a direct kick from his hands.

GOALS – MOST IN A CAREER

LEAGUE		OVERALL	
1 Eric Brook	158	1 Eric Brook	177
1 Tom Johnson	158	2 Tom Johnson	166
3 Billy Meredith	145	3 Colin Bell	152
4 Joe Hayes	142	3 Joe Hayes	152
5 Billy Gillespie	126	5 Billy Meredith	151
6 Tommy Browell	122	6 Francis Lee	143
7 Horace Barnes	120	7 Tommy Browell	139
8 Colin Bell	117	8 Billy Gillespie	132
9 Frank Roberts	115	8 Fred Tilson	132
10 Francis Lee	112	10 Frank Roberts	128

GOALS – MOST IN A CUP MATCH

TEAM – 12–0 v Liverpool Stanley 4 October 1890
FA Cup Qualifying Round One
INDIVIDUAL – 6 Denis Law v Luton Town 28 January
1961
FA Cup Round Four (match abandoned)

GOALS – MOST IN A LEAGUE MATCH

TEAM – 11–3 v Lincoln City 23 March 1895 (h)
Division Two
INDIVIDUAL – 5 Tommy Johnson v Everton
15 September 1928 (a)
Division One (game won 6–2)
5 George Smith v Newport County
14 June 1947 (h)
Divison Two (game won 5–1)

GOALS – MOST IN A SEASON

TEAM – 108 Division Two 1926/27, team finished third.
(In 1937/38, City scored more goals (80) than
any other side in Division One, but were still
relegated.)
INDIVIDUAL – 38 Tom Johnson Division One 1928/29

GODWIN, HARRY, Following his demob in 1945, Harry Godwin tried to rekindle his amateur playing days with Salford Newbury. At half-time in his first comeback game, a derisory remark from referee Fred Daniels, (a supposed friend), caused Harry to think differently about his playing career.

Already well known in the amateur game as a man with sound judgement of players, Godwin received an offer in 1949 from a former City player Jack Boothway. Boothway's offer was on behalf of his close friend Les McDowall, then manager at Wrexham, and so began Godwin's career, albeit initially on a part-time basis, which would eventually see him become one of the games' most respected talent spotters.

In 1949, Godwin moved to Second Division Bury, before again joining forces with McDowall, this time at Maine Road, and still as a part-timer, in 1950.

He spent the next fifteen years scouting for the Blues on this part-time basis, finally being offered a full-time contract in March 1965. Within four days of him becoming a full-timer, (and turning down similar offers from Leeds United and Stoke City), manager George Poyser was sacked and Godwin's job hung in the balance.

New boss Joe Mercer quickly reassured Godwin that his job was safe, and would later give him the title of chief scout.

For the next nine years, up until his retirement from ill health in 1974, Godwin would bring more than 40 players from literally nowhere to become first team regulars at Maine Road. Players such as Stan Bowles, Tommy Booth, Joe Corrigan and Tony Towers were spotted by the eagle eyes of Harry Godwin.

Following his retirement, Godwin reverted back to his part-time hours, giving him ample time to spend talking football with, and supplying endless sweets to, any youngster interested in football.

Affectionately known as 'Uncle Harry' by hundreds of Junior Blues, Harry Godwin passed away on 24 September 1993.

GOODCHILD, JIM, born Southampton, 4 April 1892. A steady rather than spectacular goalkeeper, Jim Goodchild arrived at Hyde Road on 2 December 1911 from Southampton.

Walter Smith was City's first choice 'keeper at the time, and after much competition for places, Goodchild became the number one at the start of the 1915/16 season.

His debut had come in a 2–0 defeat at Aston Villa on 20 January 1912, and before a move to Guildford City on 18 August 1927, he played in 216 league and cup games for the Blues. During his time with City he won an FA Cup runners'-up medal, after defeat by Bolton Wanderers in 1926.

His fifteen-year career with City however, might never have happened. Goodchild was discarded by Southampton after just five senior appearances, and took a job as a docker in his home town. Fortunately, for Goodchild, and City, word reached Hyde Road that a possible goalkeeping talent was going to waste.

GORTON AFC. Gorton Association Football Club was the combined name of two other local sides, West Gorton, and Gorton Athletic.

At the beginning of the 1884/85 season, the newly formed club joined the Manchester and District Association. In October 1884, a rent of £6 per annum secured a pitch on Pink Bank Lane, close to Belle Vue. This pitch was only minutes walk from the Kirkmanshulme Cricket Club ground where West Gorton had previously played their matches.

West Gorton had initially been the brainchild of the Reverend Arthur Connell, vicar of St. Mark's Parish, and two church wardens, Messrs. Beastow and Goodyeare. There were still links between the church and the new club, indeed Mr Beastow was made honorary vice-chairman, and it was he who presented the club with their first strip. This was made up of all black shirts with a large white cross on the front.

Gorton AFC were to play just one season (16 games, won seven, lost two, drawn seven), on Pink Bank Lane, before moving to rented land behind the Bull's Head Hotel on Reddish Lane. Games played on this ground were described as 'rough' and 'very bad conditions', and a rent review by the landlord in the summer of 1887 forced the club not only to change grounds, but to change area, and therefore the club name. (See Ardwick FC.)

GRAY, MATT, born Renfrew, 11 July 1936. Manager Les McDowall returned to Scottish club Third Lanark to sign inside-forward Matt Gray on 26 February 1963. It was only five months earlier that the same club had sold Alex Harley to City, and the two Scots joined forces for the first time in City's colours in a 2–1 home win over Birmingham on 2 March 1963.

Gray's arrival at Maine Road coincided with a welcome change in the weather, as a severe icy spell had prevented the Blues from playing any games since 15 December the previous year.

City were relegated at the end of Gray's first season, which saw him score six goals in 18 league appearances. In all, Gray scored 23 goals in 97 (+4) league and cup appearances during his time at Maine Road, and on 17 April 1967, he moved to Port Elizabeth in South Africa.

The highlight of his career with City was probably a Boxing Day hat-trick scored in the 8–1 demolition of Scunthorpe United in 1963.

GROENENDIJK, ALFONS, born Leiden, Holland, 17 May 1964. A left-sided midfielder with a UEFA Cup winners' medal to his name, Groenendijk arrived at Maine Road on 23 July 1993 from top Dutch side Ajax.

Having played 16 times in Europe, a fee of £500,000 was required to bring this experience to City, manager Peter Reid looking at ways to strengthen his senior squad. Groenendijk had earlier played for Roda JC Kerkrade in the Dutch league, and in his first season in England, he played a total of just 12 games in City's first team. Unfortunately for Groenendijk, things didn't work out for him in England, and on 24 August 1994 he returned to Holland when he joined Sparta Rotterdam for a fee of £100,000.

GROUNDS. Under their various earlier names, Manchester City have played at the following grounds:

1880–1881 Clowes Street
1881–1882 Kirkmanshulme Cricket Club
1882–1884 Queen's Road/Clemington Park – 'Donkey Common'
1884–1885 Pink Bank Lane
1885–1887 The Bull's Head Hotel
1887–1923 Hyde Road
1923 – present Maine Road

H

HAMILL, MICKEY, born Belfast, 19 January 1885. Formerly a player with Manchester United under Ernest Mangnall, Mickey Hamill was recalled from his native Belfast when Mangnall, now manager at Hyde Road, remembered his talents on 29 September 1920.

At United he had been an inside-forward, but City converted him into a wing-half, and it was in this position that he broke into the Irish team in 1921 for the first of seven caps. Although an exceptionally talented footballer, Hamill's laid-back attitude and lack of stamina prevented him from becoming a better and more inspirational player.

He spent four seasons with City, scoring twice in 128 league and cup appearances, before emigrating to the United States where he joined Boston side Fall River in 1924.

Hamill later returned to Ireland to manage Distillery, but suffered a tragic end when his body was fished out of a canal in mysterious circumstances, in July 1943.

HANNAH, GEORGE, born Liverpool, 11 December 1928. After being rejected by Everton, George Hannah spent the early part of his career in Irish football. A move to Newcastle United in September 1949 provided the launch pad for Hannah, and he scored 41 times in 167 league games for the Magpies, before signing for Lincoln City in September 1957.

Hannah had actually scored for Newcastle against City in the 1955 FA Cup final, and he signed for the Blues on 19 September 1958 for a fee of £20,000. His debut came the following day in a 4–1 defeat at Highbury, and despite a frail-looking appearance, he would become a City regular for the next six seasons.

Hannah's skill on the ball often shone through in a City side that struggled throughout his time at Maine Road. On 10 July 1964, after 131 league and cup games, with 16 goals, £2,000 took Hannah to Notts. County.

HARLEY, ALEX, born Glasgow, 20 April 1936. Alex Harley spent less than a year at Maine Road, but the impact he made was immense.

He had hit 71 goals in two seasons to top the Scottish scoring charts for his club Third Lanark, and City did well to acquire his services for a bargain £19,500 on 24 August 1962.

His debut came in the third game of the 1962/63 season, a 2–0 home defeat by Aston Villa. (The first game of that season saw the Blues lose 8–1 at Wolves. Even City's consolation that day was an own goal.)

An out and out centre-forward, Harley quickly settled into a scoring groove, and within three weeks of his arrival, he established a hero status by grabbing a last-minute winner in the derby at Old Trafford.

Harley's goals became legendary with City fans, and he scored again in the return derby at Maine Road later that season, when a disputed last gasp penalty by Albert Quixall salvaged a point for United. Despite the Scot's prodigious efforts, a remarkable 23 goals in just 40 league games, the Blues found themselves relegated at the end of Harley's debut season.

On 14 August 1963, Harley moved to Birmingham City for a fee of £42,000. He played 28 league games for Birmingham before spells with Dundee and Leicester, and he even played a short time in South Africa.

THE MAINE ROAD ENCYCLOPEDIA

He was found dead in his hotel room of a suspected heart attack in 1969, whilst working as a croupier in a Birmingham casino. A tragic end to a short but colourful life.

HARPER, ALAN, born Liverpool, 1 November 1960. One of football's most versatile players, Alan Harper was Howard Kendall's first signing for City on 13 December 1989.

Harper had played for both Merseyside clubs, working with Kendall at Everton, before moving to Sheffield Wednesday in July 1988. £150,000 brought him to Maine Road from Hillsborough, and he made his City debut at Goodison Park in a goalless draw on 17 December. Always a reliable performer in any position Harper played 55 (+4) league and cup games for the Blues, scoring twice, before returning to Goodison Park on 6 August 1991.

HART, JOHNNY, born Golborne, 8 June 1928. Johnny Hart was one of the unluckiest men ever to play league football, and also one of its greatest club servants.

He made his debut as a 17-year-old in a 5–1 defeat at Sheffield Wednesday on 12 September 1945, after joining City from local football, and went on to give remarkable service at Maine Road. Unfortunately his playing career was dogged by injuries, as can be seen from the fact that he only managed 177 league and cup games in more than 13 seasons. The cruellest blow of all came in 1955 when a broken leg sustained at Huddersfield robbed him of an FA Cup final place against Newcastle.

After six operations, Hart recovered sufficiently enough to regain his first team place, but, in only his fifth league game back, he suffered further injuries which would eventually force him to retire.

On 29 August 1956, he broke four ribs and had a lung punctured in a collision with Tottenham's Ted Ditchburn during a league match at White Hart Lane. Such were the severeties of these injuries, Hart himself later commented that he thought he was dying.

Understandably he never really recovered from these injuries, playing only six more league games before finally calling it a day on 4 May 1963.

During his playing time at Maine Road, he had topped City's scoring charts on three occasions, and his goal tally of 73 from an abbreviated career showed just what might have been achieved but for those injuries.

Retirement, however, was not the end of Hart's Maine Road career. He joined City's backroom staff and served the club admirably in a variety of roles for over a decade, including trainer and then, briefly, manager in 1973, before the pressures of the job and nervous exhaustion caused him to quit the post after only six months. Johnny Hart, the epitome of the loyal one club man, was rewarded with a long service presentation in 1969 and a testimonial match in May 1974.

HARTFORD, ASA, born Clydebank, 24 October 1950. In 1972, after more than five years and 206 (+8) league games for West Bromwich Albion, Asa Hartford looked all set to sign for the might of Don Revie's Leeds United.

This transfer fell through when a medical report discovered Hartford had a hole in the heart. Because of this, Leeds decided not to take a chance, but, on 13 August 1974, City did take a chance, and a fee of £210,000 secured Hartford for the Blues. His first City debut came four days later in a 4–0 home win against West Ham United.

For the next five years, this fiery Scot was the midfield engine room for City, and he won 36 of his Scotland caps whilst at Maine Road.

On 27 June 1979 Hartford moved to Nottingham Forest for twice the fee that City had bought him for. He played just three league games for Forest before being transferred to Everton where he stayed for more than two years.

On 1 October 1981, Hartford signed again for the Blues, this time for £375,000, making his second debut in a goalless Maine Road derby on 10 October.

His second spell consisted of 75 league appearances, and on 8 May 1984, he left Maine Road for the sunnier climate of NASL side Fort Lauderdale Sun.

On his return to England, Hartford joined Norwich City, and after spells with Bolton, Stockport County, Oldham and Shrewsbury, he joined the coaching staff of Stoke City.

In July 1995 Asa Hartford once again returned to Maine Road, this time as assistant manager to the newly appointed Alan Ball.

HAT-TRICKS
The following is a list of City's top ten scorers of hat-tricks:

	League	Other	Total
Fred Tilson	7	4	11
Horace Barnes	4	7	11
Tommy Browell	6	4	10
James Currier	–	10	10
Billy Meredith	6	3	9
Tom Johnson	4	5	9
Eric Brook	4	4	8
Billy Gillespie	4	3	7
Peter Doherty	3	4	7
Alex Herd	1	6	7

Detailed below, are the clubs who have conceded the most hat-tricks when playing against City:

	League	Others	Total
Stockport County	–	11	11
Everton	7	3	10
Preston North End	6	3	9
Aston Villa	6	1	7
Blackburn Rovers	4	3	7
Liverpool	4	3	7
Bury	3	4	7
Leyton Orient	5	1	6
Bolton Wanderers	3	3	6

HAYES, JOE, born Kearsley, 20 January 1936. A former colliery and cotton mill worker, Joe Hayes was invited for trials by City after impressing scouts in local football in and around Bolton.

The impact he made in that trial – he scored four times – convinced the Blues to sign him. This they did, on 29 August 1953, and within the space of eight weeks, Hayes had made his first team debut, albeit in a 3–0 defeat at Tottenham. At that time, he was still three months short of

*Kearsley-born Joe Hayes who scored 152 goals in 363 first team games
for the Blues, including one at Wembley in the 1956 FA Cup final
(News Team International)*

his 18th birthday, and he played only eleven times during
his first season.

The following season Hayes scored 15 goals in 26 league
and cup games, and City realised they had discovered one of
the greatest goalscorers of his era.

Despite being fairly small for a forward, only 5'8" and
suffering from poor eyesight, Joe Hayes would eventually
score 152 goals in 363 senior outings for City. He won an
FA Cup winners' medal in 1956 as the Blues beat
Birmingham (Hayes incidentally scoring the opening goal
that day), and was the proud recipient of two Under-23
honours for England.

On 28 December 1964, when still only 28, Hayes suffered
a serious knee injury in a collision with Bury goalkeeper
Chris Harker during a league match at Gigg Lane.
Unfortunately for Hayes, and City, he never fully recovered

from the injury, and on 30 June the following year he left Maine Road for Barnsley.

HEATH, ADRIAN, born Stoke, 11 January 1960. When Howard Kendall signed the 5'6" Heath for City on 20 February 1990, it was the third time that the two men had joined forces. Stoke City and Everton were the two previous clubs, and following a brief spell with Spanish side Espanol, Heath had moved to Aston Villa in August 1989. It was from here that this England B international arrived at Maine Road, to join the seemingly ever growing Everton contingent. Because of his size, Heath was often a handful for taller central defenders, and on occasion proved the perfect foil for Niall Quinn. He made his debut for City as a substitute in a 2–1 defeat at Charlton Athletic on 24 February 1990, and played a total of 68 (+20) games, scoring six times, before returning to Stoke on 26 March 1992.

HENDRY, COLIN, born Keith, 7 December 1965. Described by a TV commentator as 'a stormtrooper of a centre-half', Colin Hendry had played 102 league games for Blackburn Rovers when he signed for City on 10 November 1989.

Prior to Blackburn, he had played 41 times for Dundee, and his debut for City was easily forgotten as the Blues went down 3–0 at Nottingham Forest on 18 November.

His effort, commitment, defensive capabilities, and his ability to score the odd goal, made Hendry an instant favourite with the fans. So much so that he won the much coveted Player of the Year trophy at the end of his first season.

Despite all these qualities, new manager Peter Reid was to spend £2.5 million on Keith Curle in August 1991, and Hendry realised his days were numbered. After just five substitute appearances in the 1991/92 season, the frustrated Hendry returned to Ewood Park, where he eventually won international recognition with Scotland.

Still popular at Maine Road, Hendry played 70 (+7) times for City, scoring ten times.

HERD, ALEX, born Bowhill, 8 November 1911. Two FA Cup final appearances inside 15 months were Alex Herd's reward for a move to City from Hamilton Academicals on 1 February 1933. He went on to win First and Second Division Championship medals in a 15-year stay at Maine Road, and would eventually make 283 league and cup appearances for the club, scoring 120 goals.

A strong running inside-forward with a powerful shot, Herd probably lost his peak years to the Second World War, although it was during that time that he did play for the Scottish League.

He moved to Stockport County on 16 March 1948 on a free transfer, and whilst at Edgeley Park he achieved a remarkable family feat when he turned out in the same side as his son David, in a 1950/51 league match against Hartlepool United.

Alex Herd died in 1982 at the age of 70.

HESLOP, GEORGE, born Wallsend, 1 July 1940. Given the chance of regular first team football by City after years of virtual obscurity with his first two league clubs, Newcastle and Everton, George Heslop seized the opportunity with relish.

Joe Mercer paid Everton £20,000 on 14 September 1965 for the services of the big, blond centre-half, and under the influence of Mercer and Allison he became a key member of the City team which swept all before them. During his time at Maine Road, Heslop won League Cup and European Cup Winners' Cup medals to go alongside Championship honours in both the First and Second Divisions.

His one league goal in a City career spanning 195 (+6) appearances could not have been more vital, coming as it did in a 3–1 victory at Old Trafford which set the Blues on course for their Championship success of 1967/68.

George Heslop spent a year on loan in South African football before leaving City permanently on 11 August 1972 to join nearby Bury. In more recent times, Heslop was the landlord of The City Gates pub, formerly The Hyde Road Hotel, which although now derelict, still stands adjacent to the former ground of Ardwick FC.

HILL, ANDY, born Maltby, 20 January 1965. Full-back Andy Hill began his career as an apprentice at Old Trafford, although he never actually played in United's first team.

In July 1984, he moved to Bury, where he was to make 264 league appearances, winning promotion with the Shakers the following year.

Nearly seven years' experience and consistently good performances brought Hill to the attention of manager Peter Reid, who paid £200,000 for him on 18 December 1990. He had to wait until 16 March 1991 for his first team debut, a 1–1 draw at home to Wimbledon, although he had been a regular feature on the subs' bench.

He wore the number three shirt for that Wimbledon game, but it has been at number two that he has turned in many unsung performances to date for the Blues.

HILL, FREDDIE, born Sheffield, 17 January 1940. Anyone who saw Freddie Hill not wearing a football kit would never believe he could make a living playing professionally. This, however, he most certainly did for over 17 years, winning England caps at both Under-23 and full level into the bargain. The trademark stooping run saw him through 410 league and cup games over 12 years for Bolton, before a move to Halifax Town in July 1969. Joe Mercer and £10,000 brought him to Maine Road on 4 May 1970, and his debut came at The Dell in the opening game of the 1970/71 season.

His creative play and tremendous passing ability created many chances for his team-mates, and in his final season at Maine Road he played largely in the reserves, always willing to pass on his extensive knowledge.

Hill scored three times in 33 (+7) first team appearances, as well as four times in 51 reserve team outings. On 25 May 1973, he moved to Peterborough United where he was to play 73 (+2) games before a spell in non-league football.

HILLMAN, JACK, born Tavistock, 30 June 1870. A remarkable, eccentric character who gave substance to the old adage that 'all goalkeepers have to be crazy', Jack Hillman joined City from Burnley on 21 January 1902. Over the next five seasons he gave outstanding service and entertainment, during which time he won a Second Division Championship and an FA Cup winners' medal.

A Devonian who was larger than life in all respects, Hillman stood six feet tall and weighed over 16 stones, second only to Sheffield United's giant 'Fatty' Foulke as the country's largest goalkeeper. Admired greatly by the supporters of the day, Hillman once won a bet by keeping goal one-handed in a charity match in Scotland, where he had spent the early part of his career playing for Dundee.

After 124 league and cup appearances, Jack Hillman was ordered by the FA to be discarded by City in the aftermath of their investigation in 1906. He moved briefly to London where his career was ended at Millwall by a serious elbow injury which left him with a crooked arm in later life.

HINCHCLIFFE, ANDY, born Manchester, 5 February 1969. The young City side that won the FA Youth Cup in 1986, provided many players that would eventually progress into the first team. Left-back Andy Hinchcliffe was one of these players.

Signed originally on apprentice forms in July 1985, Hinchcliffe turned professional in February the following year. Mel Machin gave him his first team opportunity in the opening game of the 1987/88 season, one that the 18-year-old grasped with both hands, playing in 42 of the 44 league games that season.

On 11 July 1990, after 134 (+5) senior appearances, Hinchcliffe moved to Goodison Park in a deal which brought Neil Pointon to Maine Road. Of his 11 goals for City, none will be more memorable than the final one in the famous 5–1 derby victory on 23 September 1989.

HODGE, PETER, born Dunfermline. On 24 April 1926, City lost 1–0 in the FA Cup final to Bolton Wanderers. Further disappointment followed eight days later when the Blues were relegated. In between times, David Ashworth had left the club, and Peter Hodge took over the manager's chair. Hodge had experience at Dunfermline and Raith Rovers, before moving south to Stoke City, then a non-league side, in 1914. After the First World War, he spent

THE MAINE ROAD ENCYCLOPEDIA

seven years at Leicester City where he guided them into the First Division.

Hodge's first season at Maine Road came desperately close to a First Division return. The Blues won their last game of the season 8–0, taking their tally for the season to 108, only to lose out on promotion by 1/200th of a goal to Portsmouth. The next season, 1927/28, City won the Second Division Championship, beating Leeds United into second place by two clear points.

City finished eighth, third, fourth and 14th over the next four seasons, during which time players of the calibre of Brook and Toseland had signed for the Blues.

In March 1932, Hodge, tempted by a long-term contract and a higher salary, returned to Leicester, with club secretary Wilf Wild being promoted to manager.

HOLDEN, RICK, born Skipton, 9 September 1964. Initially spotted by Burnley whilst at teacher training college, Rick Holden played only one first team game before moving to Halifax Town in September 1986. 83 (+1) appearances later, he joined Watford for a fee of £125,000 in March 1988. Holden returned north, this time to Oldham Athletic, in August 1989, where he was a key man in a successful side that enjoyed good cup runs and won promotion to the First Division.

It was Holden's skill down the left wing, and his high level of 'assists', that prompted Peter Reid to sign him on 5 August 1992 in a player/cash deal which saw Steve Redmond and Neil Pointon move to Boundary Park. The idea was to provide better service for Niall Quinn, but Holden found it difficult to reproduce his form on a regular basis, and on 11 October 1993, after 57 (+1) first team appearances and five goals, he returned to Oldham.

HORTON, BRIAN, born Hednesford, 4 February 1949. City's 18th manager since the end of World War Two, took over the reins following the dismissal of Peter Reid in August 1993.

At the time of his appointment, Maine Road was experiencing some difficult times, and although he had been

a professional for over 16 years, and manager of Oxford
United, to say he was unknown to Blues' followers was
somewhat of an understatement. His previous encounter
with City was as a member of the fateful Luton side which
won at Maine Road in the last game of the 1982/83 season.

City's first game under Horton was a 3–1 victory at
Swindon, but a crippling injury list, many of them long
term, meant he was forced to battle against relegation for
the bulk of his first season. Never one to avoid criticism or
media interviews whatever the result, Horton's forthright
attitude won over the support of the fans quickly, and new
chairman Francis Lee also pledged his support, and much
needed cash, for the manager following his successful
takeover of the club in February 1994.

The 1994/95 season proved another disappointing one
for City. They finished two places above the relegated clubs,
and, just three days after the last game, the chairman's
support ran out and Horton was dismissed. He was the 12th
Premier League manager to lose his job either during, or
just after, that 1994/95 season.

HUNDRED GOALS IN A SEASON. The magical figure
of 100 goals in a season has been achieved by the Blues on
four occasions:
  1926/27 108 goals – Final position 3rd in Division Two
  1927/28 100 goals – Final position 1st in Division Two
  1936/37 107 goals – Final position 1st in Division One
  1957/58 104 goals – Final position 5th in Division One
All the above seasons were played over 42 games.

In 1926/27, Middlesbrough won the Second Division
with 122 goals.

In 1957/58, Wolves won the First Division with 103
goals, whilst Preston finished second with 100. The neutral
supporter must have loved watching City that season. Not
only did they score 104, but they also conceded 100. The
Blues had three 5–2 victories and one 6–2, but suffered a
total of 15 defeats, including a 9–2 and an 8–4.

HUNDRED THOUSAND POUNDS TRANSFER. On
13 July 1961, City sold Denis Law to Italian side Torino for

£110,000. This was the first time a British club had been involved in a transfer deal involving £100,000 or more.

Twelve months later, Law returned to Manchester, this time to Old Trafford for £115,000, to provide United with the record of being the first British club to buy a player for a six figure sum.

The first time the Blues spent £100,000 on a player was on 8 March 1972. In typical City fashion, they actually doubled that, when Malcolm Allison paid £200,000 for the talents of Rodney Marsh. City's previous highest purchase was £65,000 for Arthur Mann on 25 November 1968.

HUTCHISON, TOMMY, born Cardenden, 22 September 1947. Capped seventeen times for Scotland, Tommy Hutchison's name will always be associated with the 1981 FA Cup final.

During that first drawn game with Spurs, Hutchison, the oldest player on the pitch, emulated the feat of Charlton Athletic's Bert Turner in 1946, when he scored for both teams.

A skilful and tricky left-winger with tremendous experience, Hutchison had played for Alloa Athletic, Blackpool and Coventry City, (312 full league appearances), before arriving at Maine Road on 22 October 1980.

He was one of John Bond's first signings, along with Coventry teammate Bobby McDonald, as the new manager sought to steady the sinking Maine Road ship. Hutchison's debut came in the 2–1 home victory against Brighton & HA three days after his signing, and he played a total of 57 (+3) games, scoring five times, before a move to Hong Kong side Bulova on 1 July 1982.

On his return to England, Hutchison joined Burnley, where he played 92 league games before a further move to Swansea in July 1985.

I

INGEBRIGTSEN, KAARE, born Trondheim, Norway, 11 November 1965. The second Norwegian after Aage Hareide to appear on City's books, Ingebrigtsen initially came to Maine Road on a trial period in December 1992.

A midfield player with international experience, Ingebrigtsen so impressed manager Peter Reid that he was offered a permanent position on 25 January 1993. Norwegian First Division club Rosenborg Trondheim received £500,000 from the Blues, and Ingebrigtsen's debut came as a substitute in the 3–2 home win over Blackburn Rovers just five days after signing.

During the summer of 1993, following a disagreement with Reid, Ingebrigtsen returned to his former club on loan. New manager Brian Horton brought him back to Maine Road, and on 8 January 1994, Ingebrigtsen rewarded him with a 3rd round FA Cup hat-trick against Leicester City. Since May 1994 he has been back in Norway on loan to various clubs.

INTERNATIONAL MATCHES AT MAINE ROAD. Since the end of the Second World War, just two international matches have taken place at Maine Road. They were:

13 November 1946   England 3 Wales 0
16 November 1949   England 9 Northern Ireland 2
                              (World Cup qualifier)

J

JEFFRIES, DEREK, born Manchester, 22 March 1951. Following his successes with both Manchester and Lancashire schoolboys, Longsight-born Jeffries signed professional forms for City on 1 August 1968. He had been on City's books since 22 July 1966 as an apprentice, and it was during this time that he made his way into the Central League side.

His first appearance in the senior side was as a substitute for Francis Lee in a 2–1 home victory against West Bromwich Albion on 4 October 1969.

A talented, if occasionally casual looking central defender, he had a habit of trying to dribble his way out of trouble when the 'big boot' was the safe and easy option, and in total he played 82 (+10) league and cup games before being transferred to Crystal Palace on 24 September 1973.

During his time at Maine Road, Jeffries never scored for City, although he did manage a spectacular 25-yard own goal past Joe Corrigan in a game against Southampton on 16 December 1972.

JOHNSON, TOM, born Dalton-in-Furness, 19 August 1901. The credit for Tom Johnson's move to City on 22 February 1919 must go to Eli Fletcher, the Blues' outstanding left-back at the time, who refused to re-sign for the club if they did not buy Johnson from his local club Dalton Casuals.

Fletcher's judgement of the talented youngster proved spot on. Johnson scored on his debut for the Blues against Blackburn Rovers at Hyde Road on 22 February, and followed that up with a hat-trick against Port Vale in the next home game two weeks later.

It was the launch of a spectacular City career which was to span 11 seasons and see him play 353 league and cup games, and score 166 goals, his individual haul of 38 goals in the 1928/29 season still being a club record.

During his time with City, Johnson played in the 1926 FA Cup final, and in the side that won promotion in 1927/28. He also earned two England caps, and represented both the Football League and the Football Assocation.

On 5 March 1930, the Maine Road management believed him to be past his best and they sold him to Everton for £8,000. Johnson proved them wrong by winning Second and First Division Championship medals at Goodison Park, and three more England caps. A further irony was that Johnson was in the Everton side that beat City 3–0 in the 1933 FA Cup final.

JOHNSTONE, BOBBY, born Selkirk, 7 September 1929. Bobby Johnstone was a member of the 'Famous Five' forward line in the fabulous Hibernian side of the early '50s which won three Scottish Championships and finished runners-up on a further three occasions.

The star-studded attack of Gordon Smith, Johnstone, Lawrie Reilly, Willie Ormond and Eddie Turnbull broke the stranglehold imposed by Celtic and Rangers north of the border, and Johnstone was already an established international when City paid the Easter Road club £20,700 for his services on 2 March 1955.

His brilliant ball skills soon earned him cult status on the Maine Road terraces, as the City faithful realised he posssessed a huge talent. Within 14 months of his signing, Johnstone had played in two successive FA Cup finals for the club and scored in both – the first man ever to achieve this feat.

Scottish forward Bobby Johnstone – the first man ever to score in successive FA Cup finals, in 1955 and 1956

He nearly missed the 1956 victory over Birmingham due to injury, but played with pain-killing injections and a heavily strapped thigh. Despite these difficulties, Johnstone managed to score the third goal for City which effectively took the game out of the Midlanders' reach.

As well as 17 Scottish caps, four earned whilst at Maine Road, Johnstone also represented Great Britain against a Rest of Europe select, and was respected throughout the game as one of the best players of his type in the country.

After 137 league and cup appearances for City, and 50 goals, Johnstone re-signed for Hibs on 22 September 1959 for a fee of £3,000. He later returned to the north west with Oldham Athletic where he scored 35 times in 143 league games.

JONES, WILLY LOT, born Chirk, April 1882. A regular member of the renowned Welsh international side of the early 1900s, Willy Lot Jones was a native of Chirk, the same town that produced his legendary countryman Billy Meredith. He joined City from Rushton Druids on 19 January 1903, and played in just one game during his first season. He would eventually play in 300 league and cup matches in a variety of forward positions, winning a Second Division Championship medal in 1909/10.

Despite 75 goals for City, he was regarded as somewhat of an erratic finisher who should have hit the net on many more occasions.

He won all bar two of his 20 Welsh caps whilst with City, before joining Southend United in August 1919. When his playing career had finished, he managed several Welsh sides, including Wrexham and Oswestry.

Jones ran a chain of successful grocery shops in Chirk until his death in the town on 13 July 1941.

JUNIOR BLUES. Quite rightly, Manchester City Football Club is proud of its Junior Blues Organisation.

Originally a germ of an idea in the mind of Malcolm Allison, the organisation really began to develop in 1973, when Peter Swales became club chairman. Its main aims were to foster good football-supporting disciplines for juniors and to encourage friendliness with other clubs' junior supporters organisations.

Within a short period of time the initial membership of 200 had risen to 7000, and such was the success of the organisation, that by 1988, 75 per cent of the 92 league clubs had contacted City in order to improve their own junior organisations.

To date, the Junior Blues has had over 30,000 members, many from outside Great Britain, with the current membership in the region of 4,000. Monthly meetings are held in the Social Club at the ground where members get the chance to meet players, play games, take part in competitions, etc. A full-colour quarterly magazine is also produced, and the organisation provides all the ballboys for first team games at Maine Road.

Anyone interested in joining the Junior Blues should contact the organisation's secretary, at the club.

K

KENDALL, HOWARD, born Ryton-on-Tyne, 22 May 1946. As a player, Howard Kendall displayed his midfield talents in over 600 league games, in a career spanning 18 years and six clubs. His appearance at Wembley in 1964, when he was just 17, made him at the time, the youngest player to appear in an FA Cup final.

Kendall's managerial career began at Blackburn as player/manager, moving to Goodison Park in 1981. The following six years produced two League titles, the FA Cup and the European Cup Winners' Cup. These successes, when added to three other Wembley appearances, made Kendall one of the top managers of the '80s. In June 1987, he left Everton to take up a challenging position with Spanish side Atletico Bilbao, but was dismissed in November two years later after a disappointing run of results.

On 11 December 1989, following the departure of Mel Machin, Howard Kendall took charge at Maine Road, becoming the club's 17th manager since the end of World War Two.

At the time of his arrival, City were languishing near the bottom of the First Division. Within a matter of weeks, Kendall, after some shrewd transfer dealings, had steadied things, and the Blues eventually finished the season in a creditable 14th position.

On 6 November the following year, City, after just one defeat in the opening 11 games of the season, were rocked when Kendall resigned and returned to his 'first love', Everton. A decision which angered many City fans, and for which he will probably never be forgiven.

KENNEDY, BOBBY, born Motherwell, 23 June 1937. Bobby Kennedy was already a big success in Scottish football when City paid £45,000, at that time a record fee for a wing-half, to obtain his services from Kilmarnock.

He had overcome serious illness in his career to help Killie twice become Scottish Cup finalists, and also League runners-up, before moving south to Maine Road on 20 July 1961.

Kennedy joined City in the same week as Peter Dobing, as the club tried to pacify supporters upset by the sale of Denis Law to Torino, and came with the reputation of possessing a thunderbolt shot and an enormous throw-in. This reputation was enhanced when he scored a spectacular goal on his City debut against Leicester on 19 August 1961.

A stocky and swarthy individual, Kennedy spent eight years with the club, and despite playing throughout one of City's particularly dark periods, proved a loyal and reliable servant with nine goals in 251 (+3) league and cup appearances.

His Maine Road career survived the advent of Mercer and Allison, who converted him to a full-back role that earned him a much deserved Second Division Championship medal in 1965/66.

On 3 March 1969, Kennedy left Maine Road to become player/manager with Grimsby Town, but was the subject of mistaken identity whilst on tour with the Blues in the summer of 1968. City, as Champions, and ambassadors of the English game, were playing a series of games in the United States, and manager Joe Mercer had enforced a 10.00 pm curfew.

Sharing the same name with a famous American politician, City Chairman Albert Alexander thought it was this Bobby Kennedy who had been shot. On hearing the story on the 11.00 pm TV news, Albert said 'Well, it's his own fault for being out so late.'

KERNAGHAN, ALAN, born Otley, 25 April 1967. When Alan Kernaghan signed for City for £1.6 million on 17 September 1993, he could not possibly have expected the reaction of the crowd.

He was Brian Horton's first signing, and his debut came in a 1–0 defeat at Wimbledon just three days after joining the Blues. Largely due to injuries, Kernaghan played 30 (+1) league games during his first season, in the majority of which he suffered crowd abuse almost from before the first whistle. By his own admission, Kernaghan's performances were not up to standard, and a vicious circle was started, when, in an attempt to play better and therefore win over the fans, he began to play more cautiously, which inevitably led to more mistakes.

To improve both his game and his shattered confidence, Kernaghan spent time on loan with Bolton Wanderers at the start of the 1994/95 season. A central-defender who had played over 200 league games for Middlesbrough as well as being capped for the Republic of Ireland, he was determined to make a success of his career at Maine Road. Players with less heart would have asked for a transfer.

Almost immediately following his return to first team action, the crowd were witnessing a new player. He was more confident and dominant, and his overall performances got better and better. The joy on his face after he had scored his first league goal for City (at Southampton on 4 February 1995), hopefully means that the bad times are over.

KEVAN, DEREK, born Ripon, 6 March 1935. On 22 August 1963, following City's relegation at the end of the previous season, new manager George Poyser bought Chelsea's unsettled inside-forward Derek Kevan for £35,000.

Kevan had played only seven league games for Chelsea since joining them from West Bromwich Albion, where he had scored an amazing 157 goals in 262 league games. Poyser hoped that these goalscoring feats could be repeated for City, and Kevan did not disappoint, with 30 goals

THE MAINE ROAD ENCYCLOPEDIA

coming in 40 league games in his first season. A hat-trick against Norwich City at Easter time was included in these 30, and his partnership with Jimmy Murray (21 goals in 19 games), caused considerable difficulties for most defences.

He scored 18 times in 27 games in the 1964/65 season before a knee injury sustained at Derby on 30 January forced him to miss the rest of the season.

On 29 July 1965, Kevan, who had also scored eight times in 14 appearances for England, moved to Crystal Palace. Further spells at Peterborough, Luton and Stockport preceded his time as landlord of the Moss Rose public house on the doorstep of Macclesfield Town AFC.

KIDD, BRIAN, born Manchester, 29 May 1949. Signed on apprentice forms by Manchester United, Brian Kidd scored 70 goals in 274 appearances before being transferred to Arsenal in July 1974. Perhaps his most famous goal for United came on his 19th birthday in the 1968 European Cup triumph over Benfica.

On 7 July 1976, manager Tony Book signed Kidd for the Blues for a fee of £110,000. He made his debut for City in a 2–2 away draw at Leicester on 21 August, but had to wait until 30 October for his first league goal, away at Norwich City.

In his two full seasons at Maine Road, City finished second and fourth in Division One, with Kidd scoring 37 times, including four in one game against Leicester City on 22 January 1977.

On 29 March 1979, Kidd moved to Everton for a fee of £150,000, after a Maine Road career of 57 goals in 127 (+1) league and cup appearances.

Following Everton, Kidd played with Bolton Wanderers, before moving to the NASL with firstly Atlanta Chiefs, and then Fort Lauderdale Strikers. On his return to England, he was manager briefly at Preston, before linking up with Alex Ferguson for a successful partnership at Old Trafford.

KINKLADZE, GEORGIOU, born Tblisi, Georgia, 6 July 1973. This 21-year-old Georgian international midfielder signed for the Blues on 14 July 1995. Dynamo Tblisi were the recipients of a $3 million fee (approx £2 million), and he arrived at Maine Road on the same day as new manager Alan Ball.

Kinkladze had been the outstanding player in a Georgian side which beat Wales 5–0 in the qualifying round of the European Championship. He scored in that game, and also in the return leg in Cardiff where he chipped Neville Southall for what turned out to be the spectacular winner.

Already a fan of the English Premier League and its players, Kinkladze had interested Chairman Francis Lee for six months prior to his signing, and the player himself is well aware of the different style of play in England.

The speed of his signing forced Ball to allow him to return to Dynamo Tblisi for ten days' training with his former team-mates prior to the commencement of the new season. Ball, like Lee, is convinced Kinkladze has both the necessary skill and adaptability to be a big success in English football.

He will certainly get tremendous support from the City faithful.

KINSEY, STEVE, born Manchester, 2 January 1963. Former Manchester Boy and England Youth International, Steve Kinsey signed professional forms for the Blues on his 17th birthday, with his first team debut coming in a 3–1 victory at Wolverhampton on 18 April 1981.

The Gorton-born Kinsey represented England Youth in the Little World Cup in Australia in 1980, and holds the unusual record of being voted City's Young Player of the Year in 1980, 1981 and 1982.

He wore a number of different shirts during his 5½ years at Maine Road, but he was at his most happiest when playing up front. Two short loan spells with Chester and Chesterfield in 1982 increased his experience, and he played in 33 (+2) games of City's 1984/85 promotion season.

On 11 October 1986, Kinsey left Maine Road, like so many before, and after, for a spell in the United States. He played for Minnesota Kicks and Tacoma before joining Rochdale on a non-contract basis in October 1991.

He scored 17 times in 97 (+17) league and cup appearances for City, and was also on the score sheet in the 1986 Full Members' Cup Final at Wembley.

L

LAKE, PAUL, born Manchester, 28 October 1968. Already the proud owner of England Under-21 and B international caps, Paul Lake would certainly have played many times for the full England side but for a horrendous knee injury sustained in September 1990.

This injury kept him out of the game for almost two years, and more tragedy was to strike on his return to first team action.

On 19 August 1992, only eight minutes into City's second game of the season, an away game at Middlesbrough, Lake again damaged his cruciate knee ligaments. This injury meant more surgery, this time in the United States, and, to date, Lake has not yet played again in the senior side.

Denton born, Lake was another member of City's tremendous youth side of the mid '80s, who signed schoolboy forms in 1982. Apprentice forms followed, before he turned professional in June 1987.

A sparse Wimbledon crowd of 5,667 saw Lake's first team debut on 24 January 1987, and he played in only three games that season. It was the following season, 1987/88 that he really established himself. He played 30 league games that term, with manager Mel Machin asking him to wear nine different shirts.

To date Lake has played 130 (+4) league and cup games for the Blues, and scored 11 times. A left-sided midfield player of tremendous ability, he has undoubtedly saved the club millions of pounds in the transfer market.

LAW, DENIS, born Aberdeen, 24 February 1940. It was fortunate for the game of football, that it was the late, great, Bill Shankly who brought Denis Law to England.

A man with less knowledge and vision than Shankly, would have turned away the small, thin schoolboy with bad eyesight who arrived in Huddersfield in February 1957.

Shankly saw at this early stage what crowds all over the world were to see for the next 17 years. Law would spend nearly three years at Leeds Road, scoring 16 times in 81 league appearances.

On 15 March 1960, City manager Les McDowall smashed the existing British transfer record by £10,000, when he paid Huddersfield £55,000 for Law's services. This made Law Britain's first £50,000 player, and, as with many of the game's great goalscorers, he scored on his debut for his new club. The Blues lost 4–3 at Elland Road on 19 March, and Law scored again in his next game eleven days later. In the following season, 1960/61, Law was City's leading scorer in the league, with 19 goals from 37 appearances. This was also the season when he scored an amazing six times in the abandoned FA Cup tie at Luton.

On 13 July 1961, Law became Britain's first £100,000 footballer (actually £110,000), when he moved to Italian giants Torino. Arriving in Italy at the same time as fellow Scot Joe Baker, Law survived just one Italian season, and a car crash, before returning to England in August 1962. Another £100,000 changed hands, as Manchester United became the first British club to buy a player for a six-figure sum.

Undoubtedly the best part of Denis Law's career was spent at Old Trafford, winning league and cup medals, but missing out through injury on the 1968 European Cup Final.

On 2 July 1973, after 171 league goals in 305 (+4) appearances, he was given a free transfer by United, and

City manager Johnny Hart had no hesitation in bringing him back to Maine Road.

As on his first City debut 13 years earlier, Law scored again, this time twice, as the Blues beat Birmingham 3–1 on the opening game of the 1973/74 season. A forward line of Summerbee, Bell, Lee, Law and Marsh, saw City through to Wembley for the final of the League Cup, only for a 2–1 defeat by Wolves.

The last day of the 1973/74 season proved to be the worst of Law's long and illustrious career. He scored City's goal in the 1–0 victory at Old Trafford, a goal which effectively relegated United to the Second Division. He never kicked a ball again in league football. Following two World Cup appearances in the summer of 1974, Denis Law finally retired on 26 August.

Now a respected TV soccer pundit, one of the world's most famous, and greatest players, scored 37 times in 77 (+2) league and cup appearances during his two spells at Maine Road. Unfortunately for Law, and City, the six scored at Luton are not eligible for inclusion in these figures.

LEAGUE POINTS – HIGHEST. In an attempt to reward attacking football, the Football League decided from the start of the 1981/82 season, to award three points instead of two for a win.

With this in mind, City's best seasons are:

Pre 1981/82   62 points in the 1946/47 season

Analysis –	P	W	D	L	F	A
	42	26	10	6	78	35

Position – Champions Division Two

Since 1981/82   82 points in the 1988/89 season

Analysis –	P	W	D	L	F	A
	46	23	13	10	77	53

Position – Second in Division Two

LEAGUE POINTS – LOWEST. Using the same criteria as in the previous entry, City's worst season is:

Pre 1981/82   18 points in the 1893/94 season, the last of Ardwick FC.

Analysis –

P	W	D	L	F	A
28	8	2	18	47	71

Position – 13th in Division Two

Since 1981/82   39 points in the 1986/87 season

Analysis –

P	W	D	L	F	A
42	8	15	19	36	57

Position – 21st (relegated) in Division One

These figures do not include the expunged 1939/40 season.

LEE, FRANCIS, born Westhoughton, 29 April 1944. When Francis Lee signed for City for £60,000 on 9 October 1967, he had already scored 92 goals in 189 league games for Bolton Wanderers. He made his debut for Bolton as a 16-year-old on 15 November 1960, against City, and scored, forming a partnership with another future City player, Freddie Hill.

Lee's debut for the Blues came in a 2–0 home win over Wolves on 14 October, and his arrival at Maine Road coincided with an unbeaten run of 11 games. That first season saw Lee score 16 times in 31 league appearances, and he was undoubtedly the final piece in the Mercer and Allison puzzle that brought the Championship to Maine Road for the first time in over 30 years.

Lee's bustling, fearless style of play earned him the first of his 27 international caps (England losing only three times in those 27 games), against Bulgaria on 11 December 1968, and he was top scorer in five of his seven trophy-packed seasons at Maine Road. His most prolific season was 1971/72 when he scored 35 times, including a record 15 'Lee One Pen' penalties.

Even as a youngster, Lee had a good head for business, and all the time he was playing football, he was amassing considerable assets from a thriving wastepaper business.

On 14 August 1974, after 143 league and cup goals for City, placing him sixth overall, much to the horror and disappointment of City's supporters, Lee was transferred to Derby County for £110,000.

Wastepaper millionaire, professional footballer, racehorse owner and present chairman of Manchester City Football Club, Francis Lee (News Team International)

Lee himself was angered by the club's decision, and he promised at the time that Maine Road had not seen the last of Francis Lee.

He played two seasons with Derby, where he won a second Championship medal, scoring 24 times, including a tremendous effort at Maine Road, before retiring at the end of the 1975/76 season. Thought by many to be a premature decision, he was still only 32, Lee had decided to concentrate entirely on his business interests. In 1986, these stretched to horseracing, when he obtained an owner-trainer's licence.

Francis Lee's comments in August 1974, finally came to fruition when, in February 1994, he did indeed return to Maine Road. After many weeks of legal wranglings, he was finally named as chairman of Manchester City. Always the crowd's favourite, both on and off the pitch, 'Franny' began a long, hard task to restore the good times to Maine Road.

All those involved with Manchester City know if any one man can do it, then Francis Lee is that man.

LEIVERS, BILL, born Bolsover, 29 January 1932. Bill Leivers turned down the chance to move to several clubs before City finally persuaded him to leave Third Division North Chesterfield.

A fee of £8,000, on 27 November 1953, brought this country boy to Maine Road, and once over his big city settling in period, he forced his way into the first team. Once established, he showed himself to be a tough, reliable defender who was to give City excellent service for over a decade, playing in 281 league and cup games.

Standing 6ft 2in tall and weighing 13 stones, Leivers was a centre-half by trade, but featured mainly as a right-back during his early years at Maine Road, and he won an FA Cup winners' medal in 1956 whilst wearing the number two shirt.

Later in his career he reverted to centre-half at a time when City were struggling and heading for relegation, and throughout remained a fierce competitor.

A catalogue of injuries, including no less than five broken noses, a broken ankle and a broken elbow, bore testimony to Bill Leiver's bravery as a City stalwart.

He left Maine Road for a fee of £1,000 on 10 July 1964 to join Doncaster Rovers as player/manager. After Doncaster, he took his forthright managerial methods to four other lower division clubs, the most successful being Cambridge United, who won the Southern League twice, and gained entry to the Football League under his leadership.

LITTLE, ROY, born Manchester, 1 June 1931. Full-back Roy Little joined City on 6 August 1949 from amateur side Greenwood Victoria.

His career spanned just over nine years at Maine Road, though he had to wait until 17 January 1953 for his league debut, a 3–1 away win against Liverpool. He played three times that season, but really established himself the following year when he played in 31 of the 42 league games. The only two goals of Little's Maine Road career of 186 league and cup games came in that 1953/54 season.

Little played in the successive FA Cup final sides of the mid '50s, collecting a winners' medal in 1956, before a move to Brighton & HA on 18 October 1958. He later played for Crystal Palace before becoming player/manager of Southern league side, Dover.

LIVINGSTONE, GEORGE, born Dumbarton, 5 May 1876. A crowd of 16,000 saw the opening game of the 1903/4 season as City won 2–1 at Stoke City.

New signing George Livingstone made his City debut in that game, and scored the first of his 20 goals for the club.

A player of great experience, he had played previously for, amongst others, Celtic and Liverpool (from whom he joined City), Livingstone proved to be an outstanding member of the Blues' fine team of that era.

With City he won an FA Cup winners' medal and earned the first of his two Scottish caps. Livingstone's main claim to fame was as inside-forward and chief provider to Billy Meredith, indeed it was Livingstone's through ball which Meredith ran onto to score the Cup winning goal against Bolton at Crystal Palace.

His short but brilliant career at Hyde Road ended after just 88 appearances, when in 1906, he was one of the players suspended by the FA following their investigations into alleged illegal payments and bonuses.

In January 1907, Livingstone moved to Glasgow Rangers, but would later return to Manchester when he joined rivals United.

LOMAS, STEVE, born Hanover, Germany, 18 January 1974. As a 15-year-old schoolboy, midfielder Steve Lomas played for Coleraine's first team in Northern Ireland.

He signed professional forms for City on his 17th birthday, and has since performed well in both the youth and reserve sides. Lomas played in 29 reserve team games of the 1992/93 season, and his regular good performances forced him into first-team reckoning for a pre-season tour to Holland.

The injury problems suffered by manager Brian Horton during the 1993/94 season provided an opportunity for

Lomas, one which he duly took on 25 September, in a 1–0 away win at Sheffied United.

The continuing injury problems, sometimes with eight first team regulars missing, meant Lomas was able to make 22 (+7) league and cup appearances during his debut season, in which time he also won his first cap for Northern Ireland. Lomas himself admits to benefiting enormously from playing alongside the vastly experienced Steve McMahon, and since McMahon's move to Swindon in October 1994, Lomas has assumed more midfield responsibility which, if anything, has improved his all round play.

His progress was interrupted when a double injury sustained at Crystal Palace in January 1995 caused him to miss the rest of the season.

M

McADAMS, BILLY, born Belfast, 20 January 1934. The owner of 15 Northern Ireland caps, Billy McAdams was another of those unlucky players who suffered a spate of injuries that curtailed his career.

He joined City from Irish side Distillery on 6 December 1953, and quickly made his mark with a hat-trick in only his second game for the club, a 5–2 FA Cup win at Bradford.

McAdams' cavalier forward play made him a popular figure with the Maine Road crowd, but his rugged style and bravery brought repeated back problems that cost him a regular place in the team, and he missed out on both of City's FA Cup finals in the mid 1950s. The 1959/60 season saw him earn an extended run in the first team, and he prospered with 21 goals from only 30 league appearances to finish as the club's top scorer for the season.

It came as a surprise, therefore, that on 2 September 1960, McAdams was sold to Bolton Wanderers for a fee of £25,000. His seven seasons at Maine Road had produced 62 goals from 134 league and cup games. After Bolton, McAdams had a spell with Leeds United before becoming a prolific goalscorer in the lower divisions with teams such as Brentford and Queen's Park Rangers.

McCARTHY, MICK, born Barnsley, 7 February 1959. A tough, uncompromising centre-half, typical of the breed, Mick McCarthy played 272 league games for his home town club before signing for City on 14 December 1983.

His debut came three days later in a dour goalless draw at Cambridge. Signed as a replacement for Tommy Caton, McCarthy's regular solid performances made him the supporters' choice for Player of the Year at the end of his first season at Maine Road. It was during this same year that he won the first of his 57 caps for his adopted Republic of Ireland.

On 20 May 1987, after 163 league and cup appearances with three goals, McCarthy moved to Celtic, where he won League and Cup winners' medals, for a fee of £500,000. After leaving Parkhead, he tried his luck in Europe, spending two seasons with French club Olympique Lyon, before joining Milwall in March 1990.

He captained Ireland in the Italia World Cup, and in March 1992, he became player/manager at Millwall when Bruce Rioch moved to Bolton.

McCLOY, PHIL, born Uddingston, April 1896. Phil McCloy was one half of a Scottish international full-back pairing with Ayr United club mate Jock Smith, when City paid £3,000 for his services on 27 August 1925.

Described as the calmer of the two, McCloy struggled initially to adjust to the pace of English football, and the new offside rule in particular. Once these difficulties had been overcome, McCloy settled down to become a regular first teamer, and would win a Second Division Championship medal in 1927/28, to go with his 1926 FA Cup runners-up medal.

On 4 August 1932, after 157 league and cup appearances, he left Maine Road for a spell in Irish football. Phil McCloy died in 1972, aged 76.

McDONALD, BOBBY, born Aberdeen, 13 April 1955. Signed with team-mate Tommy Hutchison on 22 October 1980, Bobby McDonald brought to an unsettled City side, the experience of exactly 200 league games, firstly with Aston Villa and then Coventry City.

As all City fans will remember, that 1980/81 season saw a great turnaround in the club's fortunes, as they finished 12th in the league, and were beaten FA Cup finalists.

McDonald's debut came in a 2–1 home victory over Brighton on 25 October, and he finished the season with seven goals from 36 league and cup games. 'Sarge' continued with steady, dependable performances over the next two seasons, carrying on in the same vein as previous left-backs Glyn Pardoe and Willie Donachie.

Prior to the start of the 1983/84 season, McDonald and manager Billy McNeill came to a disagreement over a point of club discipline. This led to the player being sold to Oxford United on 9 September, where he would play nearly a hundred league games, before spells with Leeds United, Wolves and non-league Burton Albion.

Whilst on City's books, Bobby McDonald scored 16 times in 111 (+1) first team appearances.

McDOWALL, LES, born Gunga Pur, India, 25 October 1912. The son of a Scottish missionary, former aircraft draughtsman Les McDowall was spotted by Sunderland whilst playing with other unemployed workers during the hard times of the 1930s.

He played only 13 times in three seasons at Roker Park before joining City on 14 March 1938 for a fee of £7,000. His arrival at Maine Road couldn't prevent the Blues from being relegated in his first season, but the following season, the last before World War Two, saw McDowall made captain and play in all but four league games.

During the war, McDowall was able to return to draughtsmanship, a career which gave him enough time to play in 122 wartime games for City. The 1946/47 season saw the resumption of normal football, as well as the Blues' return to the First Division, although by now, McDowall had relinquished the captaincy to Sam Barkas.

In November 1949, after a Maine Road career spanning 123 games with seven goals, McDowall became player/manager of Wrexham. Within eight months, he was back at Maine Road, this time as manager, and his first job was once again to restore First Division football.

This he duly did, at the first season of asking, and a successful 13-year managerial career had begun. During those 13 years, the Blues appeared in two FA Cup finals, and introduced 'The Revie Plan' to British football. McDowall was responsible for signing City favourites such as Denis Law, Dave Ewing and Colin Barlow, but in June 1963, following relegation at the end of the previous season, McDowall left Maine Road to take over at Oldham Athletic.

City's longest serving post-war manager Les McDowall died in August 1991 at the age of 78.

McILROY, SAMMY, born Belfast, 2 August 1954. Capped 88 times for Northern Ireland, midfielder Sammy McIlroy began his career at Old Trafford as an apprentice in July 1969. After 342 league games, he moved to Stoke City where he played a further 133 league games, before arriving at Maine Road on 1 August 1985.

McIlroy scored on his debut for City, a 1–1 draw at Coventry on the opening day of the 1985/86 season, but an Achilles injury sustained after just ten games, meant he missed all but the last two matches of the season.

He made only one appearance the following season, also against Coventry, before moving to Oergryte Gothenburg of Sweden on loan. At the end of this loan period, McIlroy returned to the north-west, where he joined Bury, this time on a permanent contract, on 4 March 1987.

Another spell in Europe, this time with Austrian side V.f.B. Modling, followed, before he became player/coach at Preston in February 1990. By this time, McIlroy's thoughts had turned more to management, and he would leave Deepdale to become player/manager with Northwich Victoria. At the time of writing, Sammy McIlroy is manager of Macclesfield Town.

MacKENZIE, STEVE, born Romford, 23 November 1961. On 27 July 1979, the flamboyant Malcolm Allison, now in his second term as City manager, spent £250,000 on a 17-year-old yet to make his Football League debut.

Steven MacKenzie was this player, tipped by Allison to become one of England's finest over the next few years.

MacKenzie arrived at Maine Road from Crystal Palace, where he was on apprentice forms, and made his debut, alongside other City newcomer Michael Robinson, in the opening game of the 1979/80 season. More than 40,000 saw the game, a goalless draw, coincidentally at Crystal Palace.

He scored twice in 17 (+2) league appearances that season, but City struggled throughout, spending long periods at the bottom end of the table, as well as suffering an embarrassing 3rd round FA Cup defeat at Fourth Division Halifax Town.

The following season proved better for both club and player. After Allison's departure in October, new manager John Bond steadied the ship, and the Blues finished 12th in the league and beaten FA Cup finalists. MacKenzie made 47 league and cup appearances that season, scoring eight goals, including one of the best ever seen at Wembley, as City lost in a replay to Spurs.

On 13 August 1981, Mackenzie was transferred to West Bromwich Albion, but was back at Maine Road 16 days later, making his debut for his new club. The holder of England honours at Youth, Under-21 and B level spent nearly six years at The Hawthorns, before playing at Charlton, Sheffield Wednesday and Shrewsbury.

McMAHON, STEVE, born Liverpool, 20 August 1961. A midfielder of great tenacity and experience, Steve McMahon arrived at Maine Road on Christmas Eve 1991.

A £900,000 signing from Liverpool, McMahon had played in more than 200 league games, winning three Championship medals and 17 England caps during his time at Anfield.

He made his debut for City in a 2–1 home win over Norwich City on Boxing Day, just five days after playing in a Liverpool side held 2–2 by the Blues on Merseyside. His arrival at Maine Road instilled the missing bite into the side, a statement that also applies to any side he has played in since making his league debut as an 18-year-old for Everton back in August 1980.

His tackling and passing ability quickly made him popular with the fans, and his experience greatly influenced the younger players such as Garry Flitcroft and Steve Lomas. McMahon played in 94 (+4) games for the Blues, with just one goal, before the presence of these youngsters forced him out of the side in September 1994.

At the age of 33, McMahon, a fully qualified coach, began to look around for a new position, and on 28 November he became player/manager of First Division Swindon Town. Showing no shortage of the old aggression, McMahon managed to get himself sent off in only his second appearance for his new club, but did have the satisfaction of taking his side to the semi-final of the Football League Cup in only his first season in charge.

McMULLAN, JIMMY, born Denny, 26 March 1895. An uncle to Matt Busby, Jimmy McMullan was captain of the Scottish side dubbed 'The Wembley Wizards' after they had handed England a 5–1 drubbing in 1928.

A skilful wing-half who had begun his career with the famous Denny Hibs, McMullan was already an established international when City signed him from Partick Thistle on 10 February 1926 for £4,700. Described as a 'superb tactician', he gave sterling service to the club over the next eight seasons, clocking up 238 league and cup appearances with 8 goals.

He won a Second Division Championship medal in 1927/28, and during his time at Maine Road, he appeared in two FA Cup finals, against Bolton and Everton. Much to his bitter disappointment, he finished on the losing side in both games, and he left the field in tears after the defeat by Everton in 1933.

Sixteen days after that Everton game, the 38-year-old McMullan had left Maine Road to become player/manager with Oldham Athletic. He would later manage Aston Villa and Notts County before being dismissed by Sheffield Wednesday in 1942. Jimmy McMullan died in Sheffield on 28 November 1964.

McNAB, NEIL, born Greenock, 4 June 1957. Currently in charge of City's A team, Neil McNab was Billy McNeill's first signing for the Blues on 20 July 1983.

His career had begun with Morton before moving south to Tottenham in February 1974, and he had played at Bolton, Brighton and Leeds (on loan) before £35,000 brought him to Maine Road.

His debut for City came in the opening game of the 1983/84 season, a 2–0 home victory over Crystal Palace, and he played 33 league games that season, scoring just the one goal, a token gesture as the Blues let in five at Fulham. Injuries meant he could only play in 15 (+3) games the following season as the Blues won promotion back to Division One. The next four seasons saw City relegated again, and promoted again, Trevor Morley's goal at Bradford in the last game of the 1988/89 season proving vital.

McNab played in 42 of City's 46 league games that season, and such was his overall presence in the side, that he won the Player of the Year award.

On 4 January 1990, after 260 (+5) league and cup games, and 19 goals, McNab moved to Tranmere Rovers for £125,000, where he would make two Wembley appearances.

More recently he has played for several non-league clubs, including Witton Albion, before returning to Maine Road in his present position in the summer of 1994.

McNEILL, BILLY, MBE, born Bellshill, 2 March 1940. After a record-breaking career of 831 games for Celtic, Billy McNeill became manager of Clyde in April 1977.

As a player he collected nine Scottish League winners' medals, seven Scottish FA Cup Winners' medals, six Scottish League Cup Winners' medals, and in 1967, a European Cup Winners' medal. In 1974 he was awarded the MBE for services to football, before retiring as a player in 1975.

As a manager, McNeill spent only two months at Clyde before a move to Aberdeen in June 1977. Within ten months he had moved again, this time back to his beloved Parkhead, where following the death of Jock Stein, he was to enjoy more success.

Following City's relegation at the end of the 1982/83 season, Billy McNeill arrived at Maine Road to replace the

125

beleagured John Benson. The Blues finished fourth at the end of his first season in charge, but the following season managed one place higher, and with it promotion.

During McNeill's reign, players such as Neil McNab and David Phillips arrived at Maine Road, and City lost out to Chelsea in the final of the Full Members' Cup at Wembley.

City finished 15th at the end of the 1985/86 season, and within days of the new season starting, McNeill had left for Aston Villa, leaving assistant manager Jimmy Frizzell in charge. How ironic therefore, that the 1986/87 season saw both City and Villa relegated, and McNeill was dismissed. Fortunately Lady Luck was shining on McNeill at this point as within days, Celtic had offered him his old job back.

MACHIN, MEL, born Newcastle-Under-Lyme, 16 April 1945. On 22 May 1987, Mel Machin became City's 16th post-war team manager when Jimmy Frizzell became general manager.

A man of limited managerial experience, he had previously been coach at Norwich, Machin inherited a relegated side, but within two seasons, had returned them to the top flight.

Machin's playing career lasted over 15 seasons, mainly in the lower divisions, with Port Vale, Gillingham and Bournemouth, finishing at Norwich where he played 96 league games.

He brought this experience, along with a shrewd footballing brain, to Maine Road, and some of his signings were very good indeed. Andy Dibble, Ian Bishop and Clive Allen were all signed by Machin, and they were his sides that thrashed Huddersfield Town 10–1 on 7 November 1987, and Manchester United 5–1 on 23 September two years later. This was his one and only derby, but within two months of this memorable triumph, Machin had been dismissed by chairman Peter Swales.

Howard Kendall was the new man in charge, with Machin being a supposed victim of 'unpopularity with the spectators'. 'Farmer Mel' became manager of Barnsley, where he stayed for more than three years before a surprise resignation in May 1993.

THE MAINE ROAD ENCYCLOPEDIA

MAINE ROAD. On the night of 6 November 1920, a fire caused by a cigarette end, destroyed the 4,000 seater, all wooden main stand, and club records at City's Hyde Road ground. The club mascot, an Airedale Terrier named Nell, also perished in the fire, and it was at this time that the club realised a new ground should be sought.

In the summer of 1922, after deciding against a move to Belle Vue Pleasure Park, and being told their Hyde Road ground was required for tramway improvements, City acquired a 16¼-acre site in Moss Side.

A fee of £5,500 secured the former brickworks, and top Manchester architect Charles Swain was brought in by chairman Lawrence Furniss to design a 'Wembley of the North'.

Sir R. McAlpine & Sons won the contract, and 3,000 tons of soil was brought in from a site on nearby Wilbraham Road. This soil, when placed on a foundation of cinders, provided the base (some eight feet deep) for the two-inch thick, 100-year-old Poynton turf which was to be the playing surface.

The enormous terracing, 110 steps high in some places, was accessed by six capacious tunnels, one in each corner, and two in the 'popular side'. These last two were still used up to the end of the 1993/94 season, when the Kippax Street stand was completely demolished. On 25 August 1923, a crowd of almost 60,000, entered the new ground for the first time (although the capacity was around 90,000), as City beat Sheffield United 2–1. A local newspaper at the time described the crowd as 'a many headed monster'. Only one stand, the Main Stand, was both covered and seated, and the entire stadium was built in just 300 days at a total cost of just over £100,000. Since those early days, the ground has seen many changes, both on and off the field. Without doubt, it has always been one of the country's top stadiums, and has a playing surface the envy of all visiting sides.

Let us hope that it will not be too long before fans see a return to the days of both ground and team being as great as each other.

127

MALEY, TOM, E, born Portsmouth, 8 November 1865. Within the space of four years, Tom Maley brought both good and bad times to Manchester City.

The younger brother of Celtic manager Willie Maley, Tom took over as secretary/manager of City in July 1902, after Sam Ormerod's side had been relegated at the end of the 1901/02 season.

The good times included immediate promotion back to the First Division, and positions of 2nd, 3rd and 5th in the following three seasons. FA Cup winners in 1904 (1–0 v Bolton), and over £2,000 spent on ground improvements at Hyde Road meant that City were undoubtedly one of the country's top sides during the early years of the new century.

However, all this was to change on 29 April 1905. This was the infamous day in the club's history which saw the bribe scandal rear its ugly head at Villa Park. (Full details of this are described under the 'SCANDAL' entry.)

Maley, a great advocate of the passing game, survived one further season, until being suspended *sine die*, along with the club chairman W. Forrest. A total of 17 City players were also fined varying amounts and banned from wearing City's colours again. A great period in the history of Manchester City had ended, no doubt giving enormous pleasure to the other Manchester club.

In February 1911, the FA lifted the ban, and Maley became manager of Bradford, where he stayed for 13 years, before finishing his football career with Southport in 1925. Tom Maley died in 1935, aged 70.

MANAGERS. The following is a list of team managers since 1892, the year Ardwick FC entered the league:

1889 to 1893	Lawrence Furniss
1893 to 1895	Joshua Parlby
1895 to June 1902	Sam Ormerod
June 1902 to June 1906	Tom E. Maley
June 1906 to Sep. 1912	Harry Newbould
September 1912 to May 1924	Ernest Mangnall
July 1924 to Nov. 1925	David Ashworth

April 1926 to March 1932	Peter Hodge
March 1932 to Nov. 1946	Wilf Wild
November 1946 to July 1947	Sam Cowan
November 1947 to April 1950	Jock Thomson
June 1950 to May 1963	Les McDowall
June 1963 to April 1965	George Poyser
July 1965 to Oct. 1971	Joe Mercer OBE
October 1971 to March 1973	Malcolm Allison
March 1973 to Nov. 1973	Johnny Hart
November 1973 to April 1974	Ron Saunders
April 1974 to July 1979	Tony Book
July 1979 to Oct. 1980	Malcolm Allison
October 1980 to Feb. 1983	John Bond
February 1983 to May 1983	John Benson
June 1983 to Sep. 1986	Billy McNeill MBE
October 1986 to May 1987	Jimmy Frizzell
May 1987 to Nov. 1989	Mel Machin
December 1989 to Nov. 1990	Howard Kendall
November 1990 to August 1993	Peter Reid
August 1993 to May 1995	Brian Horton
July 1995 to present	Alan Ball

MANGNALL, ERNEST, born Bolton. Ernest Mangnall became Manchester City's fifth manager when he arrived at Hyde Road in September 1912.

Blues fans must have had mixed feelings about his appointment, for the previous nine years, Mangnall had been manager of a very strong United side that had won the First Division twice as well as the FA Cup.

Having firstly been a director of his home town club, Mangnall became manager of Burnley before moving to United in September 1903. As well as the trophy successes, he would also obtain the services of Billy Meredith for United, after the Welshman had been banned from playing for City in 1906.

Mangnall's first season at Hyde Road saw a rise from 15th to sixth position in Division One, but his total of twelve years with City could not really be called glory ones. Admittedly, economically and socially, these were not the best of times, (he also had World War One to survive), but

129

he did oversee the move to Maine Road, and saw a considerable improvement in City's cash balance.

In May 1924, his contract was not renewed, and Mangnall moved back to Bolton and a place on the board of directors. A man involved in the formation of the Central League and the Football Managers' Association, Ernest Mangnall died in 1932.

MANN, ARTHUR, born Burntisland, 23 January 1948. After just 32 league appearances for Hearts, Arthur Mann joined City, then First Division Champions, on 25 November 1968.

At the time, he was City's record signing, £65,000, and he made his debut on 30 November in a 2–1 away defeat at West Ham United.

A stylish left full-back, Mann found it hard to adjust to English First Division football, particularly the speed element, and as a result played only 40 (+4) first team games, although he did play over a hundred times for the reserves.

Mann won a League Cup winners' medal during his time at Maine Road, and after a brief loan spell at Blackpool, he moved to Notts. County on 6 July 1972.

He played over 250 games for Notts. County in seven years, and in 1979, a handful of games for Shrewsbury Town. In October that year he joined his last league club Mansfield Town, where he made 116 league appearances before moving into non-league management.

MARGETSON, MARTYN, born Neath, 8 September 1971. Although currently City's third-choice goalkeeper, Martyn Margetson has won international honours with Wales at Under-21, Youth and B level. Margetson signed apprentice forms for the Blues in July 1988, with professional status being achieved two years later. His first senior appearance came on 10 October 1990, when he deputised for the injured Tony Coton in a goalless League Cup tie against Torquay United. His first full game took place on 4 May 1991, in the nerve jangling tension of an Old Trafford derby.

To date, Margetson has played in only 7 (+1) first team games, a figure which would probably have been a lot more but for the presence of Messrs. Coton and Dibble.

MARSH, RODNEY, born Hatfield, 11 October 1944. Partial deafness didn't prevent Rodney Marsh from becoming one of England's greatest ever football entertainers. His early prowess of 'cake juggling' (with his feet!) was professionally harnessed by Fulham who signed him on apprentice forms in October 1962. In March 1966, after 22 goals in 63 league games, many alongside Johnny Haynes, a man who Marsh admires greatly, he moved to Queen's Park Rangers where his reputation grew rapidly.

During his time at Loftus Road, Marsh won his first England cap, to go alongside a League Cup winners' medal, won at Wembley in 1967. Always charismatic and extrovert, Marsh scored a great solo goal in that final, and was part of a Rangers side that won promotion from the Third to the First Division in consecutive seasons.

On 8 March 1972, after 106 goals in 211 league appearances, Malcolm Allison and a club record fee of £200,000, persuaded QPR to let Marsh sign for City.

Marsh's signing came at a critical point in the season as the Blues were chasing the Championhip. City would finish the season in fourth place, and many felt that Marsh's style of play cost them the title.

His debut for City came in front of a 53,322 Maine Road crowd on 18 March, as the Blues beat Chelsea 1–0. Marsh played in seven of the remaining eight games, scoring four times, with City losing only twice. It would appear statistically anyway, that Marsh was not directly responsible for City's failure to lift the title. Even today, City fans still speculate about what might have been.

With Marsh's attitude to football being one of fun and entertainment, it was tragic that he won no club honours whilst with City, the nearest being a League Cup runners-up medal in 1974.

With his flamboyant style of play, it was perhaps no great surprise that he won only a further eight England caps during his time at Maine Road.

On 12 January 1976, Marsh, after 46 goals in 142 (+2) league and cup appearances, took his considerable talents to NASL side Tampa Bay Rowdies. He returned to Fulham in

*The flamboyant Rodney Marsh signs for City on 8 March 1972.
Witnessing the signature are (left to right) secretary Walter Griffiths,
assistant manager Malcolm Allison and chairman Eric Alexander
(News Team International)*

August that year, joining forces with his great mate George Best, for a fun-filled 16 league games.

After this brief, second flirtation with Fulham, Marsh moved back to Tampa, where he would eventually become coach and later manager. Nowadays, Rodney Marsh can be seen in theatres around the country, as he performs his stage show with George Best. Without doubt, two of football's greatest ever showmen.

MARSHALL, BOBBY, born Hucknall, 3 April 1903. A north-easterner, Bobby Marshall had an outstanding career with City after arriving at Maine Road on 1 March 1928.

He had already played 197 league games for Sunderland, where he displayed great skill and talent from an inside-forward position. He continued these performances in City's colours, and played an instrumental role in the Blues sides that reached the FA Cup finals of 1933 and 1934.

When Peter Doherty arrived at Maine Road in February 1936, Marshall was converted to centre-half, a position he challenged with great enthusiasm. This enthusiasm was rewarded with a First Division Championship medal in 1936/37.

After 351 league and cup appearances, and 78 goals, Marshall left Maine Road on 22 March 1939 to become manager of Stockport County. Marshall stayed at Edgeley Park for nearly ten years before taking over the manager's reigns at Chesterfield in February 1949.

MAY, ANDY, born Bury, 26 February 1964. A former England schoolboy, Andy May signed apprentice forms for the Blues on 23 May 1980.

Whilst still a schoolboy, he played in both legs of the 1979/80 FA Youth Cup Final, as well as in the Central League side. His first game in the senior side came on 17 April 1982, in a game which saw City go down 2–0 at Swansea.

When regular first-team left-back Bobby McDonald left Maine Road in the summer of 1983, May siezed the opportunity with both hands. New manager Billy McNeill played him in all 42 league matches that 1983/84 season, and May scored five times, including one each in both the first and last games.

In total, May played in 164 (+10) first-team games for City, including the 1986 Full Members' Cup final at Wembley, scoring nine times, as well as making exactly one hundred full appearances in the reserve side. On 3 July 1987, he moved to Huddersfield Town, before spells with Bolton, Bristol City and Millwall.

MEGSON, GARY, born Manchester, 2 May 1959. The son of former Sheffield Wednesday and Bristol Rovers full-back Don, Gary had played for five other clubs prior to joining City on 4 January 1989.

His playing career started at Plymouth, where he played 92 league and cup games, before £200,000 took him to Everton in December 1979. In August 1981, the out of favour Megson moved to Sheffield Wednesday for the first of his two spells.

A three-month period with Nottingham Forest, although no first team appearances, followed, before a move to Newcastle United in November 1984. Eleven months and 28 games later, Megson returned to Hillsborough, where he played a further 138 games before arriving at Maine Road.

His debut in a City shirt came on 14 January 1989, and it was his goal that won the game at Boundary Park. This goal proved to be half of Megson's entire league goal tally for City, his only other success coming just over two years later, the winner at Stamford Bridge on 9 February 1991.

On 1 July 1992, a free transfer enabled Megson to move to Norwich City, where, in January 1994, he was appointed assistant manager. In April the following year, he took over the manager's reins at Carrow Road following the departure of another former City player John Deehan. Megson made 90 (+5) first team appearances whilst a City player, taking him over the 500 mark since his career began.

MELLOR, IAN, born Sale, 19 February 1950. The thin, over six feet tall frame of left-winger Ian Mellor earned him the affectionate nickname of 'Spider' from the Maine Road faithful.

A former postman, he had signed amateur forms in July 1968, from nearby Wythenshawe Amateurs, and turned professional on 16 December the following year.

The injury plagued 1970/71 season was to give many City youngsters their opportunities, and Mellor's came on 20 March in a 1–1 home draw with Coventry City. He played in five further games that season, and scored his first senior goal in the last, away at Old Trafford. His first team appearances were, however, limited, and he played in 21 league games the following season, and just ten in 1972/73.

On 7 March 1973, after a total of 41 (+7) league and cup games with nine goals, and despite manager Malcolm Allison's wishes, Mellor was transferred to Norwich City.

Just over a season later, he moved to Brighton where he scored 31 times in 116 (+6) league games.

After the south coast, his career took him to Chester, Sheffield Wednesday and Bradford City. At the time of writing, Ian Mellor is back in Manchester, working as commercial manager for the PFA.

MELROSE, JIM, born Glasgow, 7 October 1958. A former Scottish Under-21 international, Jim Melrose was one of many north of the border players signed by Billy McNeill. He arrived at Maine Road on 7 November 1984, a £40,000 buy from Celtic, and his debut came six days later in a goalless draw at Sheffield United. The early days of his playing career had been spent with Partick Thistle, where he made over a hundred appearances, before moving south to Leicester in June 1980. He then had spells with Coventry City and Wolves before returning to his hometown and Celtic.

Melrose scored seven times in 23 (+1) league games in his first season with City, a season that also saw the Blues return to Division One.

On 24 March 1986, after 30 (+8) league and cup appearances and ten goals, Melrose was transferred to Charlton Athletic, where he played for nearly two seasons before moving to Leeds United and finally Shrewsbury Town.

At present Jim Melrose is manager of non-league side Bollington Athletic.

MERCER, JOE, OBE, born Ellesmere Port, 9 August 1914. Joe Mercer. The name alone not only brings back memories of the man in charge during the most successful period in City's history, but also of one of the game's most admired and respected players and men. The son of a former Nottingham Forest centre-half (also named Joe), Joe junior came into the world around the same time that World War One, and chlorine gas, effectively ended his father's playing career in the top flight.

After the war had ended, Joe senior returned to Merseyside, where he turned out regularly for the then non-league side

Joe Mercer and Malcolm Allison – 'Simply the Best'
(News Team International)

Tranmere Rovers. It was while watching his father captain the Prenton Park side, that Joe junior caught the football bug.

At every conceivable moment, the young Mercer would be playing football. Even at school, his mind was focussed on sport, and as a result, he treated his time at school as just breaks between games. Fortunately for Joe, and for English football, a new teacher, Bill Roberts, a keen football supporter, arrived at the school. Roberts was to guide and encourage Joe, and before long, Joe found himself playing for Ellesmere Port and attracting the eyes of many of the big clubs.

Everton, always Joe's favourite club, won the race for his signature when he was just 15, and the spindly, bandy legs had begun a playing career which would last for over 25 memorable years.

He won a Championship medal with Everton in 1939, before a move to Arsenal in 1946. During the war, Joe was an army PT instructor, who found time to play in 27 wartime internationals, including England's 8–0 triumph over Scotland in October 1943. (The game incidentally played in front of 60,000 at Maine Road.)

With Arsenal, Joe's reputation as a brilliant half-back continued, as did his knack of winning trophies. Two First Division titles and the FA Cup were won during his time at Highbury, and all the while Joe still lived on Merseyside.

Talk of retirement (mainly from wife Norah) had been mentioned throughout the early part of the 1950s. Joe, though, would hear none of it. However, the decision was taken out of the 39-year-old's hands on 10 April 1954. In a bizarre collision with Arsenal team mate Joe Wade, Mercer broke his leg. A magnificent playing career had ended.

A man who could not live without the game, Joe spent an uncomfortable 16 months running his successful grocery business in the Wirral before becoming manager at Sheffield United. Money restrictions and crowd dissatisfaction forced Joe to seek the vacant Aston Villa position in December 1958, where they reached two FA Cup semi-finals, and became the first ever winners of the Football League Cup.

Like Sheffield United, money was scarce, and Joe had to balance the books by selling some of the club's top players, although he did replace them with players of the calibre of Derek Dougan and Tony Hateley. In July 1964, the pressures of work finally caught up with him and he suffered a stroke.

Villa relieved him of his post, and wife Norah at last thought she had him all to herself.

How wrong could she be! On 13 July 1965, Joe Mercer, against Norah's and doctors' wishes, took over as manager of a struggling Second Division Manchester City side. Knowing full well that Joe himself was no longer fit enough for the rigours of training, his first stipulation on being appointed was that Malcolm Allison came in as his number two. In the summer of 1965, no one could possibly have known what was to come over the next seven years.

Second Division Champions, First Division Champions, FA Cup winners, League Cup winners, European Cup Winners' Cup winners, the trophies kept on coming, as Mercer and Allison (helped by some magnificent players), established Manchester City as the country's top side.

In October 1971, Allison was given responsibility for team matters, and Joe became general manager. This position meant Joe was completely uninvolved with the players, and when coupled with the internal board room wranglings taking place, proved too much. In June the following year, Coventry City offered Joe a similar position, and he moved, if somewhat reluctantly, to Highfield Road.

Following England's failure to qualify for the 1974 World Cup Finals, manager Sir Alf Ramsey was removed from the position. Without wishing to rush into a decision, the FA asked Joe if he would become caretaker manager of the national side for the next seven games. Undoubtedly this was the icing on top of a long and illustrious career.

The next few weeks saw a depressed and lacklustre England side rejuvenated. Mercer's enthusiasm and personality rubbed off on the players, who turned in some fine (and enjoyable) performances, losing just once in those seven games. Despite being offered the job on a full-time basis, Joe finally realised it was time to hang up his tracksuit for the last time.

His final few years were spent in his beloved Wirral where he spent many a Saturday afternoon watching Tranmere Rovers. Always a popular after-dinner speaker, Joe became stricken with Alzheimer's Disease, a complaint which eventually caused his death on 9 August 1990, his 76th birthday.

Without doubt, one of the game's greatest players, managers and ambassadors will never be equalled. The always smiling face belonged to a man once described by Mike Summerbee as 'the only manager of Manchester City. There will never be another like him'.

MEREDITH, BILLY, born Chirk, 30 July 1874. If W.G. Grace was the epitome of Edwardian cricket, then Billy Meredith must surely be the epitome of Edwardian football.

Perhaps the game's first 'superstar', Meredith's slender frame, bandy legs and trademark toothpick made him a cartoonists' favourite, and he was a regular feature in the newspapers of the day.

His career had begun with Welsh side Chirk, before making his debut in the English league with Northwich Victoria.

The legendary Billy Meredith – not only the oldest player to play in City's first team, but also the oldest player ever to play in the FA Cup for any team (News Team International)

In October 1894, Meredith joined City as an amateur, and became the first of eleven players who were to play in the Blues' first team with this status, when he made his debut in a 5–4 defeat at Newcastle on 27 October. Three months later, in January 1895, manager Joshua Parlby dispensed with the amateur status, and Meredith turned professional.

His career with City was in two distinct parts. The first part lasted from his signing until 1905, and the second from 1921 to 1924. During his first period with City, he won 22 Welsh caps, played 358 league and cup games, and scored 149 goals, a remarkable number for an outside right. When these goals were added to the numerous 'assists', Meredith's contribution to the Hyde Road side was immeasurable. With him in the side, City won the Second Division Championship twice, and the FA Cup, when in 1904, Meredith's goal secured victory against Bolton.

By 1905, Manchester City had become one of the top teams in the country, finishing second and third in successive seasons in Division One. It was then that Meredith was banned for nine months for allegedly trying to bribe an Aston Villa player in a vital league game.

He missed the entire 1905/06 season, and on 5 December 1906, he was transferred to Manchester United for receiving illegal payments. This same period nearly saw the end of Manchester City Football Club, as 17 players and two club officials were also suspended, and over £1,000 in fines were issued by The Football Association.

On 25 July 1921, following a wages dispute with United, Meredith, five days before his 47th birthday, returned to Hyde Road, this time as player/coach. Incidentally, whilst playing with United, Meredith had made 114 wartime appearances as a guest in a City shirt.

His second, shorter, period with City ended on 29 March 1924, when City lost 2–0 in an FA Cup semi-final to Newcastle United, the same team he had made his debut against some 29 years earlier. Meredith's amazing career with City totalled 393 games, with 151 goals, and on 29 April 1925, a crowd of 15,000 turned up for his testimonial game at Maine Road. The amazing 50-year-old played in Meredith's XI which drew 2–2 with a Rangers and Celtic XI.

After his retirement from the game, Meredith, an early advocate of a players' union, ran a pub, a cinema and a sports shop in his adopted Manchester.

On 19 April 1958, aged 82, the legendary Billy Meredith died at his home in Withington, Manchester.

MILLION-POUND PLAYERS. Up to the start of the 1995/96 season, the following players have arrived at Maine Road for a fee of at least £1 million:

PLAYER	FROM	DATE	FEE
Steve Daley	Wolves	05.09.79	£1,437,500
Kevin Reeves	Norwich City	11.03.80	1,200,000
Trevor Francis	Notts. Forest	03.09.81	1,200,000
Clive Allen	Bordeaux	14.08.89	1,100,000
Tony Coton	Watford	12.07.90	1,000,000

Keith Curle	Wimbledon	06.08.91	2,500,000
Terry Phelan	Wimbledon	24.08.92	2,500,000
Alan Kernaghan	Middlesbrough	17.09.93	1,600,000
Peter Beagrie	Everton	24.03.94	1,100,000
Nicky Summerbee	Swindon Town	22.06.94	1,500,000
Georgiou Kinkladze	Dynamo Tblisi	14.07.95	2,000,000

MORLEY, TREVOR, born Nottingham, 20 March 1962. Of all Trevor Morley's 18 league goals in 69 (+3) appearances for City, none will be remembered more than his equaliser at Bradford City on 13 May 1989. That goal gave City promotion back to Division One, and was his 12th of the season.

Signed from Northampton Town on 20 January 1988, Morley made his debut three days later in a 2–0 home defeat by Aston Villa. Prior to Northampton, Morley had spent the early part of his career with non-league Nuneaton Borough, and although his time spent at Maine Road was comparatively short, he was to have two other highlights apart from that goal at Bradford.

On 11 March 1989, he scored a hat-trick against Leicester City, and six months later, he netted the second in the famous 5–1 win over Manchester United.

Within weeks of Howard Kendall's arrival at Maine Road in December 1989, new plans had been made, and Morley, along with teammate Ian Bishop, found themselves moving to West Ham in an exchange deal which brought Mark Ward to Maine Road.

MOULDEN, PAUL, born Farnworth, 6 September 1967. As a schoolboy, Paul Moulden's goalscoring abilities not only earned him England recognition, but also a place in the *Guinness Book of Records*. Playing for Bolton Lads' Club in the 1981/82 season, Moulden scored an unbelievable 289 goals in just 40 games.

It was feats such as these that persuaded City to sign him, on apprentice forms on 4 June 1984, and on professional forms on 6 September the same year.

Once established in the first team, Moulden understandably, despite what some thought, found it

THE MAINE ROAD ENCYCLOPEDIA

difficult to maintain his scoring records, although he was leading scorer with 13 in the Blues' promotion campaign of 1988/89.

An unfortunate regular victim of injuries, including four broken legs, Moulden's Maine Road career lasted just 55 (+20) league and cup games. He found the net 23 times in those games, but on 2 August 1989, manager Mel Machin sold him to Bournemouth in an exchange deal for Ian Bishop. After less than a year on the south coast, Moulden moved back up north to spearhead the Oldham Athletic attack.

MULHEARN, KEN, born Liverpool, 16 October 1945. An apprentice with Everton before making exactly 100 league appearances for Stockport County, goalkeeper Ken Mulhearn arrived at Maine Road on 21 September 1967. Nine days later, he found himself between the posts in front of a Maine Road derby crowd of nearly 63,000, but unfortunately finished up on the losing side as United ran out 2–1 winners.

Despite this early setback, Mulhearn kept Harry Dowd out of the league side for the rest of the season, and collected a Championship medal at the end of it. Following City's disastrous exit from the European Cup in October 1968, Mulhearn, perhaps the scapegoat, was relegated to the reserves, and did not play again in the first team for over twelve months.

On 10 March 1971, the inevitable, if maybe a year later than expected happened, when, after 50 league appearances, Mulhearn left Maine Road. He signed for Shrewsbury Town, where he played nearly 400 games, before finishing his career with Crewe Alexandra in the early 1980s.

MURPHY, BILLY, 'SPUD', born St. Helens, 23 March 1895. 'Spud' Murphy was an exceptional cross-country runner who only took to football when Peasley Cross Harriers Club was disbanded at the outbreak of World War One.

As a youngster, he had earned local fame for conveying the time of arrivals of birds to headquarters while employed by pigeon fanciers.

It was this natural speed which caught the eye of City, who signed him from Alexandra Victoria on 2 February 1918. He made his first team debut on 13 September 1919, in a 4–1 defeat at Bolton, and he missed just two of the remaining 37 league games that season.

For the next six seasons, Murphy was a permanent fixture on City's left-wing, turning in a seemingly endless supply of reliable performances. At one time, he was playing so well, that the Irish FA wrote to manager Ernest Mangnall enquiring about his birthplace. They were bitterly disappointed when Mangnall informed them, that despite his name, he was a Lancashire lad from St. Helens.

After 220 league and cup appearances and 31 goals for City, Billy Murphy moved to Southampton on 18 August 1926, before returning north to Oldham Athletic.

MURRAY, JIMMY, born Dover, 11 October 1935. Ten years, 276 league appearances, 155 goals, two League Championship medals and an FA Cup winner, all with Wolves.

This was Jimmy Murray's career to date, when, on 5 November 1963, he arrived at Maine Road.

Manager George Poyser thought the striking partnership of Murray and Derek Kevan could propel the Blues back into the top division. The partnership worked immediately.

Both players scored in Murray's debut, away at Southampton on 9 November, and between them they scored 51 goals in the season. Despite these efforts, City still finished the season in sixth position.

Murray's efforts continued the following season, 13 goals in 30 league games, but the Blues fared worse, finishing eleventh.

Under new manager Joe Mercer, Murray played only 11 league games of the 1965/66 season, netting another seven goals, before a move to Walsall on 3 May 1967.

In total, he scored 46 goals, including two hat-tricks, in 78 (+1) appearances in a City shirt, and he finished his playing career in the non-league colours of Telford United.

NEWBOULD, HARRY. In the summer of 1906, the whole future and survival of Manchester City Football Club was in doubt.

The manager, chairman and 17 players had all been suspended by The Football Association following the alleged bribes scandal.

Into this hotbed situation walked new manager Harry Newbould. Somewhat surprisingly he arrived at Hyde Road from Derby County where he had been for ten years, and had built up reasonable success both on and off the field.

A former schoolboy sprinter and non-league footballer, Newbould was also a qualified accountant, training which no doubt stood him in good stead during his early days with City. In only his second game in charge, away at Everton, Newbould's side lost 9–1, a record defeat which still stands today.

Slowly but surely, Newbould began to steady the ship, and the 1907/08 season saw City finish third in Division One. The following season however, the Blues were relegated, but in typical style won promotion at the first attempt.

In July 1912, after narrowly avoiding relegation again, Newbould left Hyde Road for a coaching position in

Denmark. His links with the game continued on his return to England when he became secretary of The Players' Union, before his death in 1929.

NICKNAME. Over the years, City have been called many things by many people, most of them unprintable, but officially their nickname is either 'The Citizens' or 'The Blues'.

NIXON, ERIC, born Manchester, 4 October 1962. A former Manchester Boy, goalkeeper Eric Nixon signed for City from non-league Curzon Ashton on 9 December 1983.

As understudy to the reliable, and seemingly ever present Alex Williams, Nixon had to wait until 21 September 1985 for his first team debut, a 2–2 home draw against West Ham United. He played 41 league and cup games that season, including an appearance at Wembley, as the Blues lost 5–4 to Chelsea in the Full Members' Cup final.

The following season, Nixon played in only five league games (the last five of the season), and in July 1986 he began a series of loan moves that would take him to five different clubs. Geographically these ranged from Carlisle to Southampton, and took in all four divisions.

He regained the number one jersey for 25 league games of the 1987/88 season before signing for Tranmere Rovers, one of his loan clubs, on 26 July 1988. Nixon's Maine Road career consisted of 84 league and cup games.

NORTHERN IRELAND – FIRST CITY PLAYER. The first City player to represent Northern Ireland was outside-right Patrick Kelly.

Kelly, a former Belfast Celtic player, hailed from Kilcoo, and represented his country against England at Belfast on 22 October 1920. Sharing the wing position with an ageing Billy Meredith, Kelly scored three goals in 30 league and cup games in just under three years at Hyde Road.

O

OAKES, ALAN, born Winsford, 1 September 1942. As a player who appeared in 669 games in City's first team, Alan Oakes' loyalty and commitment to the club is second to none. It is impossible to say for certain that this club record will never be broken, but, if it is, it will take a comparable 17 seasons to do so.

The cousin of another former Blues' favourite Glyn Pardoe, Oakes signed for City as an amateur from Mid-Cheshire Boys on 8 April 1958. On 8 September the following year, he turned professional, and made his league debut against Chelsea in a 1–1 home draw on 14 November.

Oakes made 18 (+1) appearances in his first season, as he established himself as a tireless, ball-winning half-back with an excellent left foot. This left foot not only provided countless long distance balls to the right wing, but also a number of spectacular and memorable goals. None more memorable perhaps than his 30-yard strike against Atletico Bilbao in the 1970 European Cup Winners' Cup.

As his career progressed, Oakes became City's Mr Reliable and, but for the great Bobby Moore, would certainly have represented his country many times. He played for his beloved Blues through the thin times of the early 60s, and the glory days of the Mercer/Allison

146

With 665 (+4) league and cup appearances, Alan Oakes has played in more first team games for City than any other player
(News Team International)

partnership, where a medal of some description was virtually guaranteed every season.

He won his last medal in City's 1976 League Cup triumph, before leaving Maine Road on 17 July that year to become player/manager at Chester. A man who was not only a great ambassador for Manchester City, but also for English football, played 211 league games for Chester, before finishing his career, 24 years after it had started, as a coach with Port Vale.

Even today the name of Oakes is linked with top flight soccer. Alan's son Michael is currently third choice goalkeeper with Aston Villa.

OLDEST PLAYER. On 29 March 1924, City went down 2–0 to Newcastle United in an FA Cup semi-final played on Birmingham City's St. Andrews' ground. In City's side that day was the legendary 'Welsh Wizard' Billy Meredith. He was 49 years, 245 days old.

Not only is he the oldest player to appear in City's first team, he is also the oldest player ever to play in the FA Cup proper, for any side.

ORMEROD, SAM, born Accrington. A man with both playing and refereeing experience in Lancashire league football, Ormerod became City's third manager when he took over from Joshua Parlby in the summer of 1895.

At the time, he was part of a three-man managerial team, although records show that it was Ormerod who had the most influence over team matters.

At the end of the 1895/96 season, only Ormerod's second in charge, City finished second in Division Two, just missing out on promotion by heavy defeats in the Test Matches (the predecessors of today's Play Offs). Over the next two seasons, the Blues finished sixth and third, before winning the Second Division Championship for the first time in 1898/99.

The new century saw City continue in the top division, but despite the efforts of players such as Meredith and Gillespie, the club could only maintain this status for three seasons.

At the end of the 1901/02 season City were relegated. This, when coupled with a debt of over £1,000 (brought on mainly by travelling expenses and wages), forced Ormerod and City to part company. Ormerod left Hyde Road for nearby Stockport County, where he spent two years, before moving to London to manage Clapton Orient.

OWEN, BOBBY, born Farnworth, 17 October 1947. Bobby Owen will never forget his first appearance in a City shirt.

This came on 3 August 1968 with City, First Division Champions, playing FA Cup winners West Bromwich Albion in the Charity Shield game at Maine Road. A sun-drenched crowd of over 35,000 saw Owen score the first of his two goals that day within 55 seconds of the kick-off, City eventually winning 6–1.

Owen had joined the Champions from Bury on 18 July 1968, where he had scored 38 times in 81 (+2) league appearances. However he found life more difficult in the First Division, and could only manage three goals in 16 (+4) games throughout the 1968/69 season.

In March 1970, after just two more first team games. Owen moved to Swansea on loan, before signing for Carlisle United on 29 June 1970. At Carlisle he again recreated his goalscoring feats (51 in 189 (+19) league appearances), and after loan spells with Northampton, Workington and Bury, he finished his playing career with Doncaster Rovers in 1978.

OWEN, GARY, born Whiston, 7 July 1958. City fans were shocked when, on 30 May 1979, it was announced that Gary Owen had been sold to West Bromwich Albion for a fee of £550,000.

The waif-like midfielder, a home-grown favourite, was still six weeks short of his 21st birthday and was already a regular for the England under-21 side. Without doubt, Owen looked set for a key role in City's fortunes for many years to come.

He made his senior debut against Wolves at Maine Road on 20 March 1976, and established himself the following season in a Blues side that narrowly missed out on the Championship to Liverpool. Surrounded by several experienced internationals, Owen developed quickly to show a maturity beyond his years, and began to add a useful goalscoring touch to his silky, left-sided midfield skills.

He found the net 11 times in 1978/79, his best tally in what was, ironically, to be his last season at Maine Road, before Malcolm Allison's controversial decision to sell him.

Owen's career record was 122 (+2) appearances and 23 goals, though most City supporters believed it should have been many more.

P

PALMER, ROGER, born Manchester, 30 January 1959. A former Manchester Boy, and pupil at Wilbraham High School, Roger Palmer signed apprentice forms for City on 26 May 1975. On 28 February two years later, he turned professional, reward no doubt for some fine performances in the City Youth sides.

A skilful, albeit slightly built striker, he made his first-team debut in a 2–0 victory at Middlesbrough on 27 December 1977. This came in the middle of a great period of personal success for Palmer. He was voted Young Player of the Year in both 1977 and 1978, and he also picked up a Central League Winners' medal at the end of the 1977/78 season. (This was the first time the Blues had ever won this competition, and Palmer was the leading goalscorer.)

On 19 November 1980, after 11 goals in 29 (+12) first team appearances, Palmer moved to Boundary Park for a fee of £70,000. He retired in the 1994 close season having played in over 500 games for Oldham, and his goalscoring abilities have made him their record goalscorer of all time.

PARDOE, GLYN, born Winsford, 1 June 1946. Glyn Pardoe's career, spanning more than 30 years at Maine

When he was just 15 years and 314 days old, Glyn Pardoe became the
youngest player to appear in City's first team
(News Team International)

Road, was ended abruptly by then player/manager Peter
Reid, when he sacked him in May 1992. Pardoe was
coaching the reserve and youth teams, alongside Colin Bell,
and his shock dismissal upset and angered many people,
both inside and outside the club.

The cousin of another City stalwart Alan Oakes, Pardoe,
a former Mid-Cheshire and England Boy, signed apprentice
forms for the Blues on 26 July 1961. He still had that status,
when, on 11 April 1962, he made his debut in the first team.
(City losing 4–1 at home to Birmingham City.) Pardoe was
just 15 years and 314 days old, thus making him the
youngest ever player to appear in City's senior side.

During his early days at Maine Road, Pardoe was felt to
be a centre-forward, indeed he wore the number nine shirt
on his first team debut, replacing Colin Barlow. The arrival
of Mercer and Allison at Maine Road saw him converted to

151

the left-back position, where he would feature prominently during those glory years.

It was Pardoe's goal that won the 1970 League Cup for City, but, less than nine months later, his playing career was almost finished. A 4–1 league victory at Old Trafford on 12 December was tarnished when Pardoe's leg was broken in a collision with George Best. A swift operation saved the leg from amputation, but it wasn't until 4 November 1972 that fans once again saw Pardoe in the first team.

During his absence, Willie Donachie had taken over the number three shirt, so Pardoe settled for the right-back slot, before eventually retiring from playing, (after 374 (+2) appearances), on 30 April 1976.

He then became a valuable member of the club's coaching staff for 16 years before the unfortunate events of May 1992.

PARLANE, DEREK, born Helensburgh, 5 May 1953. Already a full Scottish international and trophy winner with Rangers, Derek Parlane's first English club was Leeds United, whom he joined in March 1980.

On 20 July 1983, Parlane arrived at Maine Road, via a free transfer and loan spell in Hong Kong. He made his debut on the opening day of the 1983/84 season, in a game the Blues won 2–0 at Crystal Palace.

He scored seven goals (including a hat-trick against Blackburn Rovers), in his first seven games, and played in all but two league games that debut season, finishing top scorer with 16 goals. Parlane made only seven more league appearances the following season, scoring four times, as Billy McNeill's side won promotion back to Division One. On 18 January 1985, after 23 goals in 51 (+1) games, Parlane moved to Swansea, where he played 21 league games before returning to the north-west with Rochdale in December 1986.

PARLBY, JOSHUA, In 1893, Joshua Parlby became Ardwick FC's first paid secretary/manager, receiving a mere 50 shillings a week for his trouble.

A former player and committee member with Stoke City, Parlby was at Hyde Road during the period which saw the demise of Ardwick FC, and the birth of Manchester City FC. These troubled times, with poor results and financial short-comings, proved only minor irritations to a man with Parlby's 'wheeler-dealer' qualities. It is said that Parlby would often smuggle his team onto trains (as they couldn't afford the fares) in order to travel to away matches. Despite these obvious setbacks, Parlby managed to keep City in The Football League, and during his two seasons in charge, he signed Billy Meredith, and orchestrated City's 11–3 victory over Lincoln City on 23 March 1895. This is still the club's record league victory.

Parlby handed over the managerial reins to Sam Ormerod for the beginning of the 1895/96 season, preferring instead to take a seat on the board of directors. (This probably gave him more time to run his pub in Bolton.)

In all probability, but for Joshua Parlby, Manchester City Football Club would not be in existence today.

PAUL, ROY, born Ton Pentre, 18 April 1920. As a player who won caps for Wales at all three half-back positions, Roy Paul hated to lose.

After being on the losing side to Newcastle United in the 1955 FA Cup final, Paul was so dejected, he tried to give away his losers' medal. All through that Cup campaign, Paul's thoughts were only on a winners' medal, and in the disappointment following the final, he harboured thoughts of emulating Sammy Cowan some 20 years earlier. 'Come back next year and win'. That's exactly what Paul did. Twelve months later, he had that winners' medal following City's 3–1 Wembley triumph over Birmingham City.

A former Rhondda Valley coal miner, Paul had joined Swansea in October 1938, where he played 160 league games in a war interrupted 11 years. After leaving Swansea, he decided to taste life in South America, and spent a short while playing in Colombia.

On 18 July 1950, manager Les McDowall made one of his shrewdest buys when £19,500 brought Paul to Maine Road. The Blues won promotion at the end of Paul's first season, and he missed only a handful of games over the next six

*A man who hated to lose, Welsh international Roy Paul captained the
Blues to successive FA Cup finals in the mid-1950s
(News Team International)*

seasons. A City career of 293 games and nine goals ended on
8 June 1957 when the ever dependable Paul left the Blues on
a free transfer to become player/manager of Worcester City.
He won 24 of his 33 Welsh caps whilst on City's books.

PENALTIES. Since 1919, City's leading penalty scorers are:

	PLAYED	LEAGUE	CUPS	TOTAL
1 F. Lee	1967/74	34	12	46
2 E. Brook	1928/40	29	6	35
3 D. Tueart	1974/78			
	1980/83	18	6	24
4 T. Johnson	1919/30	20	1	21
5 K. Barnes	1950/61	13	–	13
6 G. Owen	1976/79	9	1	10
6 N. McNab	1983/87	8	2	10

6 D. Revie	1951/56	8	2	10
9 M. Ward	1989/91	9	–	9
9 T. Browell	1913/26	8	1	9

PHELAN, TERRY, born Salford, 16 March 1967. A left-back with tremendous pace, Terry Phelan began his professional career, (via a YTS scheme), with Leeds United in August 1984. After only 15 (+2) first team appearances, he was given a free transfer and moved to Swansea. (At the same time, Leeds also parted company with another future Republic of Ireland full-back, Denis Irwin.) Within twelve months Phelan had moved on again, this time to 'The Crazy Gang' of Wimbledon, for what turned out to be a bargain £90,000 fee. At Wimbledon he won an FA Cup winners' medal and established himself in the Irish national side.

On 24 August 1992, Phelan became City's joint record signing when manager Peter Reid paid £2,500,000 for his services. This fee initially raised a few eyebrows, but Phelan

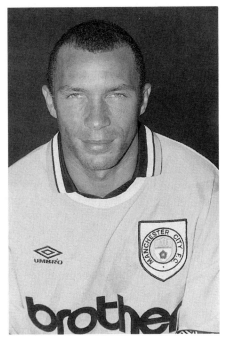

Terry Phelan (Empics Ltd)

(following his debut against Norwich City on 26 August), quickly settled into the side, and his consistent performances made him a great favourite with the fans.

Scorer of a memorable goal against Spurs in the 1992/93 FA Cup defeat at Maine Road, Phelan was a member of Jack Charlton's side during the 1994 World Cup in America.

PHILLIPS, DAVID, born Wegberg, Germany, 29 July 1963. Midfielder David Phillips signed for City on 26 July 1984 from Plymouth Argyle, and made his debut in the opening game of the 1984/85 season, a 2–2 draw at Wimbledon.

For his first three games, he wore the number two shirt, but in all bar one of the remaining 39 fixtures, he reverted to his normal midfield slot, wearing number six. (Phillips was one of three players who played in all 42 league games of that promotion season, the other two being Williams and Power.) He was also joint top scorer that season, 12 with Gordon Smith.

Although born in Germany where his father was a motor mechanic with the RAF, Phillips is eligible to play for Wales, where he has won caps at Youth, Under-21 and full level.

39 League appearances in the 1985/86 season provided just one goal (defences proving more difficult in Division One), and on 30 May 1986 a fee of £50,000 and Perry Suckling took Phillips to Coventry City.

He scored 16 goals in 99 league and cup appearances during his time at Maine Road, and he is still proving an influential midfielder today, this time in the colours of Nottingham Forest.

PLAYED FOR BOTH MANCHESTER CLUBS. The following players have been on the books of both City and United, although some didn't play in the first team:

ALBINSON, George, BANNISTER, Jimmy, BARNES, Peter, BARRETT, Frank, BLEW, Horace, BODAK, Peter, BROAD, James, BROOMFIELD, Herbert, BUCKLEY, Frank, BULLOCK, James, BURGESS, Herbert, CAIRNS, James, CARSON, Adam, CASSIDY, James, CASSIDY, Joe, CHRISTIE, John, COYNE, Ged, DALE, Bill, DANIELS, Bernard, DAVIES, Wyn, DOUGLAS, William, FIDLER,

Dennis, FITCHETT, John, GEMMELL, Eric, GIDMAN, John, HAMILL, Mickey, HAYDOCK, Billy, HICKS, George, HILL, Andy, HURST, Daniel, JONES, Di, KIDD, Brian, KNOWLES, Frank, LANGFORD, Len, LAW, Denis, LIVINGSTONE, George, McILROY, Sammy, MEREDITH, Billy, MILARVIE, Robert, MILLAR, John, MORGAN, Hugh, OAKES, Tommy, QUIN, John, READ, Bert, REGAN, Robert, RIDDING, Bill, ROWLEY, Harry, SMITH, William, STONES, Harry, TURNBULL, Alex, WALSH, Billy, WARD, Ashley, WESTWOOD, Eric, WHELAN, Robert, WHELAN, Tony, WHITEHOUSE, James, WILLIAMS, Fred, WOODCOCK, Wilf.

PLAYER OF THE YEAR. Voted for by the supporters, the following is a complete list of winners since the 1966/67 season

1966/67 Tony Book	1981/82 Tommy Caton
1967/68 Colin Bell	1982/83 Kevin Bond
1968/69 Glyn Pardoe	1983/84 Mick McCarthy
1969/70 Francis Lee	1984/85 Paul Power
1970/71 Mike Doyle	1985/86 Kenny Clements
1971/72 Mike Summerbee	1986/87 Neil McNab
1972/73 Mike Summerbee	1987/88 Steve Redmond
1973/74 Mike Doyle	1988/89 Neil McNab
1974/75 Alan Oakes	1989/90 Colin Hendry
1975/76 Joe Corrigan	1990/91 Niall Quinn
1976/77 Dave Watson	1991/92 Tony Coton
1977/78 Joe Corrigan	1992/93 Garry Flitcroft
1978/79 Asa Hartford	1993/94 Tony Coton
1979/80 Joe Corrigan	1994/95 Uwe Rösler
1980/81 Paul Power	

POINTON, NEIL, born Warsop Vale, 28 November 1964. A tough, no-nonsense left-back, Neil Pointon arrived at Maine Road on 11 July 1990 from Everton, in a deal which saw Andy Hinchcliffe move in the opposite direction.

His debut came in the opening game of the 1990/91 season, a 3–1 defeat at Tottenham, and he missed just three games that season as the Blues finished fifth. Pointon's fierce tackling and competitive spirit won him great praise from the fans, and such was his consistency, he missed only three league games of the next season as well.

His early career had been spent at Scunthorpe, and it came as a shock to many when, after two fine seasons at Maine Road, he found himself transferred to Oldham Athletic on 5 August 1992. Again he was involved in an exchange deal, this time along with colleague Steve Redmond, as Rick Holden came to City.

Pointon scored just two goals in 90 league and cup appearances for City, his replacement in the number three jersey being the club's joint record signing, Terry Phelan.

POYSER, GEORGE, born Stanton Hill, 6 February 1910. George Poyser's first managerial position was with non-league Dover Town in 1947. As a player he had had limited success as a full-back with clubs such as Wolves, Port Vale and Mansfield, and his only honour was a Second Division Championship medal with Brentford in 1935.

After Dover, he spent six years out of the game before becoming chief coach at Wolves, and then manager at Notts. County. Following his dismissal by Notts. County in 1957, Poyser became assistant manager to Les McDowall at Maine Road, a position which also gave him scouting duties.

In June 1963, after McDowall's departure to Oldham Athletic, Poyser became manager. Unfortunately for him, this coincided with one of the most disappointing periods in the club's history. Admittedly quality players such as Murray, Kevan and Crossan did arrive during Poyser's reign, but poor performances, injury problems and cup defeats by lower division sides, finally forced him to resign on 16 April 1965. (During this period, City's lowest ever attendance, 8,015, witnessed a 2–1 defeat by Swindon Town on 16 January 1965.)

The Blues finished 11th in Division Two that 1964/65 season, and, as if to rub salt into the wounds, the First Division Championship was won by Manchester United. George Poyser died in January 1995, aged 84.

POWER, PAUL, born Manchester, 30 October 1953. With 436 (+9) league and cup appearances, placing him ninth overall, Paul Power's place as one of City's most loyal servants is assured.

Originally signed as an amateur in August 1973, the Openshaw-born Power turned professional on 17 July 1975, after finishing his law studies at Leeds Polytechnic. His debut came at Villa Park in a 1–0 defeat on 27 August 1975, and he made 14 (+5) appearances in his first season, scoring once, and wearing six different numbered shirts. The following season City finished runners-up in Division One, and Power had established himself as a strong running, left-sided midfield player, a position he was to hold for the next nine seasons. Twice voted Player of the Year, Power captained the Blues in three Wembley Cup finals (FA Cup plus replay in 1981, and the Full Members' Cup in 1986), but unfortunately never finished on a winning side.

He scored 35 goals for City, none of them more important than his semi-final winner against Ipswich Town at Villa Park during that 1981 FA Cup campaign.

On 27 June 1986, somewhat surprisingly, manager Billy McNeill sold Power to Everton, where within twelve months, he was the proud owner of a First Division Championship medal.

Nowadays, Power, always a True Blue, can be heard summarising City's games on local radio, and is still more than a capable performer when turning out for City's old boys in charity matches.

PRINGLE, CHARLIE, born Nitshill, 18 October 1894. A competitive wing-half and Scottish international, Charlie Pringle signed for City from St. Mirren on 21 June 1922, and played in all 42 league games in his debut season of 1922/23.

Pringle played in the 1926 FA Cup final defeat, as well as the promotion side of two years later, and despite his lack of inches (he stood just 5ft 7ins), proved no mean performer when deputising at centre-half in the days when most teams used a big, bustling centre-forward.

Apart from his footballing prowess, Pringle's other claim to fame was that he was the son-in-law of Billy Meredith (he had married Meredith's eldest daughter, Lily), and would eventually play in the same side as the 'Welsh Wizard'.

In the summer of 1928, Pringle left Maine Road for Manchester Central, before spells with Bradford and Lincoln City, where he won a Third Division North Championship medal. He scored only once in 215 league and cup appearances for City.

PROMOTION. Since the beginning of the 1892/93 season, City (or Ardwick), have won promotion on nine occasions.

All but 21 of these 93 seasons have been spent in the top division, whether it be the old First, or the modern day Premier League. The nine successful seasons have been:

1898/99 Champions   (after seven seasons)
1902/03 Champions   (after one season)
1909/10 Champions   (after one season)
1927/28 Champions   (after two seasons)
1946/47 Champions   (after nine seasons, although World War Two prevented any play at all in six of these, and the three games of the 1939/40 seasons are expunged)
1950/51 Runners-Up (after one season)
1965/66 Champions   (after three seasons)
1984/85 Third Place (after two seasons)
1988/89 Runners-Up (after two seasons)

Q

QUICKEST GOAL. According to official club records, the quickest goal scored by a City player in a first team game was scored in the third minute of the opening game of the 1982/83 season.

The match took place at Norwich City on 28 August 1982, and David Cross was the goalscorer. It was the first goal scored in the entire league that season, and it was Cross's debut for the Blues.

QUIGLEY, MIKE, born Manchester, 2 October 1970. A stocky, ball-winning midfield player, Mike Quigley has turned in regular fine performances in both the youth and reserve sides. These performances pushed him into the first team squad, although he never really established a regular spot.

A former Trafford Boy and YTS player, Quigley signed professional forms on 23 June 1989, but he had to wait more than two years for his first team debut. This came on 23 October 1991 in a 3–2 Zenith Data Systems Cup defeat at Sheffield Wednesday.

In July 1995, Quigley, unable to emulate fellow reserves Steve Lomas and Richard Edghill and make a permanent breakthrough into the senior side, decided to try his luck elsewhere and moved to Hull City. His Maine Road career consisted of just 4 (+9) first team appearances with no goals.

QUINN, NIALL, born Dublin, 6 October 1966. In the mid-1990s, when multi-million pound transfer fees are the norm (if not necessarily worthwhile), the £800,000 spent by Howard Kendall for Niall Quinn's services on 15 March 1990, must surely class as tremendous value for money.

Having been unable to hold down a regular first team spot with Arsenal, Quinn literally leapt at the chance to join City, and responded with a goal on his debut. (Against Chelsea at Maine Road on 23 March.)

The 6ft 3ins centre-forward scored 21 league goals in the 1990/91 season, and these goals, coupled with his 100 per cent effort and commitment, won him the Player of the Year award. Quinn's abilities as one of the game's best target men have earned him full international recognition, and he was a vital member of Jack Charlton's Ireland squad for the Italian World Cup of 1990.

A cruciate knee ligament injury sustained against Sheffield Wednesday in November 1993, forced him not only to miss the rest of the season, but also the 1994 World Cup Finals in the United States.

A player with a huge heart, Quinn sensibly put these disappointments behind him, and slowly built himself back to full fitness. These efforts were rewarded when, two months into the 1994/95 season, Quinn had returned to first team action with five goals in four games.

R

RAILWAYS. During the great age of the steam locomotive, giant engines were often named after famous football clubs.

Manchester City proved no exception, and on 13 May 1937 (no doubt to coincide with City's recent Championship success), engine number 2870, class B17, resplendent in the LNER livery, came into service.

Engine number 2871, the next to come into service, should have been named after Tottenham Hotspur. This was meant to be launched officially at an exhibition in London on 29 May, but manufacturing problems meant that the engine was not ready on time. In order to avoid embarrassment, the LNER renamed City's engine to Tottenham Hotspur. Engine number 2870 carried City's name for just two weeks.

On 11 June 1937, engine number 2871 (initially destined to be the Tottenham Hotspur), was finally ready and became the second engine to bear the name Manchester City. This engine was renumbered 1671 in February 1946, and two months later, the name Manchester City was again replaced.

This time, however, the engine became The Royal Sovereign, and she was to pull The Royal Train for the next 13 years, until being scrapped in 1959. Engine number 2870 later became The City of London, and was scrapped in 1960.

RANSON, RAY, born St. Helens, 12 June 1960. Full-back Ray Ranson is one of a group of players who have had two spells with City.

His first began as an apprentice in July 1976, eventually turning professional on 1 August two years later. Ranson made his first team debut in a goalless draw at Nottingham Forest on 23 December 1978, and played in eight games that season. The next season, 1979/80, he was the regular right-back and missed just two league games.

Steady, consistent performances over the next few years earned him international recognition at both Youth and Under-21 level before a move to Birmingham City on 15 November 1984. He spent four years at St. Andrews before joining Newcastle United in December 1988.

In January 1993, manager Peter Reid re-signed him (initially on loan), and he played in 18 games before a move to Reading at the end of the season. In both spells with the club, Ranson scored just one goal in 234 (+2) appearances.

RECORD. The early 1970s saw a music trend of pop records being released by all the top clubs. As with railway engines some 35 years earlier, City proved no exception, and released their own in 1972.

On the RCA label, the song *The Boys in Blue* (written by Godley and Creme of 10CC fame), unfortunately didn't reach number one, but in comparison to some of its contemporaries, is not that bad. The song still gets an occasional airing on the ground's public address system.

REDMOND, STEVE, born Liverpool, 2 November 1967. Despite the eyes of his hometown clubs (he was already a Liverpool and England Boy), central defender Steve Redmond signed schoolboy forms for City in October 1982.

On 26 November 1984, such was his early promise and ability, that he had turned professional. By 1986, this promise had turned into first team material (debut against Queens Park Rangers on 8 February), and he would play at Wembley in the final of the Full Members' Cup.

At this time he was still only 18, and therefore eligible to play in the FA Youth Cup. Redmond captained the Blues to success in this competition, when they beat Manchester United 3–1 in the final. The following season, 1986/87, Redmond won a Central League Championship medal whilst establishing himself in the senior side with 28 (+2) league appearances.

Over the next five years, Redmond was at the heart of City's defence (indeed he did not miss a game for three seasons), and he would be rewarded with the Player of the Year trophy in 1988, and the captaincy in 1989.

On 5 August 1992, after 283 (+4) league and cup appearances with seven goals, Redmond, along with team-mate Neil Pointon, moved to Oldham Athletic in an exchange deal that brought Rick Holden to Maine Road.

REEVES, KEVIN, born Burley, 20 October 1957. Kevin Reeves' football career went almost hand in hand with manager John Bond.

As an apprentice he had joined Bournemouth (where Bond was manager), in July 1973. In January 1977, after 20 league goals in 60 (+3) appearances, Reeves moved to Norwich City (where Bond was manager).

At Norwich, his career prospered, so much so that he won the first of his two England caps (against Bulgaria in 1979), in a career producing 37 goals in 118 (+1) league games.

On 11 March 1980, Reeves became City's second million pound player when he signed for £1,200,000. Within seven months, he would again work with Bond, when his old mentor became manager at Maine Road. His debut in a City shirt came in a 3–0 defeat at Highbury on 15 March, and he scored twice in nine games in his debut season. He won his second England cap on 20 May this year, when he played against Northern Ireland at Wembley.

Reeves played in all bar three league games of the 1980/81 season (12 goals), and scored a penalty in the FA Cup final replay against Tottenham.

After 39 goals in 157 (+1) appearances, Reeves joined Burnley (again where Bond was manager), on 8 July 1983. He scored 12 goals in 20 (+1) league games for the Turf Moor side before injury forced him to retire. He is currently assistant manager at Wrexham.

REID, NICKY, born Manchester, 30 October 1960. Nicky Reid's first team debut for City came in a UEFA Cup tie against Borussia Mönchengladbach at Maine Road on 7 March 1979.

Signed initially from amateur side Whitehall Juniors on 30 April 1977, Reid turned professional on 30 October the following year, his 18th birthday.

He was a key member of the Blues' strong youth teams of the late '70s, and the tough-tackling Davyhulme lad, captained the beaten side in the 1978/79 FA Youth Cup final. Reid's league debut came in a 2–1 defeat at Ipswich on 31 March 1979, and over the next eight seasons, he would turn in many fine performances, either at the back or in midfield.

The holder of six England Under-21 caps scored two goals in 256 (+6) first team appearances for the Blues, including the 1981 FA Cup final. His Maine Road career was interrupted by a five-month spell with NASL side Seattle Sounders in 1982, before a free transfer move to Blackburn Rovers on 6 July 1987. He later played for West Bromwich Albion, and is currently with Third Division Wycombe Wanderers.

REID, PETER, born Huyton, 20 June 1956. Peter Reid was one of the most competitive players ever to appear in English football.

The owner of six Under-21 and 13 full England caps began his career with Bolton Wanderers, where he played 222 (+3) league games over a period of eight years. In December 1982, Reid moved to Goodison Park for £60,000, and would win Championship, FA Cup and European Cup Winners' Cup medals in a career lasting six years and 228 (+6) games with The Toffees.

On many occasions his fierce tackling brought about self-inflicted injuries, although he did manage to stay fit for the 1986 Mexico World Cup Finals where he played in three games, including Maradona's infamous 'Hand of God' match. In February 1989 Reid moved to Queens Park Rangers on a free transfer. He stayed at Loftus Road for ten months before arriving at Maine Road (once again to work with Howard Kendall), on 12 December.

He was given the title of player/coach, a title he kept for less than a year, until November 1990, when, following Kendall's departure, he became City's first ever player/manager. His first season in charge saw the Blues finish in a highly creditable fifth position, but the arrival of Steve McMahon in December 1991 would see Reid playing fewer games.

He eventually retired from playing after 100 (+14) league and cup games for the Blues (with two goals), before concentrating full time on management.

On 25 August 1994, just four games into the new season, City (without a win), lost their 18th post-war manager when Reid was sacked by a combination of chairman Peter Swales and new general manager John Maddock. Out of the game for several months, Reid spent time coaching at Bury before becoming manager of Sunderland in March 1995.

RELEGATION. An unfortunate subject (one that no City supporter likes to talk about), however, the Blues have suffered this tragic fate on eight occasions. The seasons in question are:

1901/02 18th (and last, although only 16 points behind Champions Sunderland)

1908/09 19th (out of 20, despite scoring more goals than Champions Newcastle United)

1925/26 21st (out of 22. One of two clubs (along with Burnley) to concede a hundred goals in the season)

1937/38 21st (out of 22, despite scoring more goals, 80, than anyone else in the entire division)

1949/50 21st (out of 22. Only 36 goals scored in 42 league games. Roy Clarke top scorer with nine)

1962/63 21st (out of 22. Conceded 102 goals in the season. Eight in the first game, and six in the last)

1982/83 20th (out of 22. A 1–0 home defeat by Luton Town (with Brian Horton and Paul Walsh) sinks the Blues on the last day of the season)

1986/87   21st   (out of 22. As per 1949/50, only 36 goals scored in 42 league games. Imre Varadi top scorer with nine, as the Blues manage just eight wins all season)

REVIE, DON, OBE, born Middlesbrough, 10 July 1927. One of the great names of English football, Don Revie will always be remembered for two achievements. His first was as a player with 'The Revie Plan' (a tactic of employing a deep-lying centre-forward similar to the great Hungarian side of the early 1950s), and his second as a manager; his tremendous successes with Leeds United.

The once apprentice bricklayer began his playing career with Leicester City in August 1944. But for a ruptured blood vessel in his nose, Revie would certainly have played in the Leicester side beaten by Wolves in the 1949 FA Cup final.

In November that year, £20,000 took Revie to Hull City, where he played 76 league games before arriving at Maine Road on 18 October 1951 for a fee of £25,000.

After witnessing Hungary's double destruction of England, manager Les McDowall encouraged Revie's idea of a domestic version of this game plan. Playing this way, the Blues reached two consecutive FA Cup finals, losing to Newcastle United in 1955, but were successful the following year with a 3–1 win over Birmingham City. The sight of a number nine collecting throws from his goalkeeper was quite revolutionary in England at the time, and it was play like this that won Revie the PFA Footballer of the Year Award in April 1955.

On 10 November 1956, after 178 league and cup games, with 41 goals, Don Revie moved back to his native north east, with Sunderland, for £21,500. He spent two years at Roker Park before moving to Leeds in December 1958. He became player/manager in March 1961, and retired from playing in May 1963.

The next 11 years saw Revie transform Leeds from an average Second Division side into one of the strongest teams in Europe. In July 1974, after domestic and European

Don Revie – a great player and manager (News Team International)

success, Revie became manager of the England side, taking over from caretaker boss Joe Mercer.

He found the job completely different from league management and was never really succesful in the position. Despite his unhappiness in the job, it came as a great surprise when, in July 1977, he accepted a £60,000 a year post as coach to The United Arab Emirates national side. He held this position for three years before coaching a short while in Egypt.

In the late 1980s, Don Revie was struck down by motor neurone disease, and died in Edinburgh in May 1989.

ROBERTS, FRANK, born Sandbach, 3 April 1894. Frank Roberts' ratio of 128 goals in 237 league and cup games for City more than repaid his transfer fee (large at the time), of £3,400. He signed for City from Bolton Wanderers on 18 October 1922, and his goalscoring feats would eventually make him City's tenth leading marksman of all time.

His best season proved to be 1924/25 when he netted 31 goals in 38 league matches, a remarkable return which earned him the first of four England caps. This season also saw Roberts score four times as the Blues beat Liverpool 5–0 at Maine Road on 17 January.

The goals kept coming during the 1926 FA Cup campaign as well. On 20 February, Roberts was on target five times as City thrashed Crystal Palace 11-4 in the fifth round. This feat was equalled by Bobby Marshall four years later, and at present, they are the only two City players to have scored five times in a completed FA Cup tie.

He formed a formidable strike force with Browell and Johnson, but unfortunately they could not overcome Roberts' old side Bolton in the final. (The Blues going down to David Jack's solitary 77th-minute goal.)

Roberts won a Second Division Championship medal with City before a move to Manchester Central on 14 June 1929.

ROBINSON, MICHAEL, born Leicester, 12 July 1958. Michael Robinson signed for City on 25 June 1979, a £765,000 buy from Preston North End during Malcolm Allison's second term as manager. He had been at Deepdale since July 1976, and had scored 15 times in 45 (+3) league games.

Robinson's City debut came in a goalless draw at Crystal Palace in the opening game of the 1979/80 season. He played 34 (+1) league and cup games that season, and finished leading scorer with eight goals. This proved to be his one and only season at Maine Road, as, on 13 July 1980, he moved to Brighton. His later career took him to Liverpool, Queens Park Rangers and Spanish side Osasuna, where Robinson, the holder of 23 Republic of Ireland caps, would eventually settle.

RÖSLER, UWE, born Attenburg, Germany 15 November 1968. Despite being at Maine Road for little over a year, striker Uwe Rösler must surely be one of City's most popular players of all time. The 'German Bomber' signed for City on 1 June 1994, from FC Nürnberg, for £500,000 following a successful three-month loan period. His debut came in a 1–1 draw at Queens Park Rangers on 5 March 1994, and he finished the season with five goals from 12 appearances.

Rösler, the holder of five full East German caps, began the 1994/95 season with a sending off at Highbury in the opening game. By the end of January 1995, he had scored 14 times in 20 (+3) appearances (in the season), including four in one game as the Blues beat Howard Kendall's Notts. County 5–2 in the FA Cup 3rd round. He was the first player since Johnny Hart in 1953 (7–0 v Swindon Town on 10 January), to score four goals for the Blues in an FA Cup tie.

A tremendous battler who causes defences no end of problems, Rösler looks set to be one of City's best ever bargain buys.

ROYALTY. On 27 March 1920, King George V visited Hyde Road to watch a Division One game between City and Liverpool. Reports state that the crowd was between 35,000 and 40,000, and City won 2–1 thanks to two goals by Horace Barnes.

Fourteen years later, on 28 April 1934, it would be the same monarch who presented the FA Cup to City's victorious captain Sam Cowan following the 2–1 defeat of Portsmouth. (The King had also been present at the 1924 final when the Blues lost 1–0 to Bolton.)

On 20 October 1934, King George V returned to Manchester, this time to Maine Road, to join a crowd of nearly 44,000 to see City go down 1–0 to Derby County.

ROYLE, JOE, born Liverpool, 8 April 1949. Joe Royle had spent more than eight years with his first club Everton, when a serious back injury cost him his place in the first team and threatened his entire career.

City took a chance on his fitness and rescued him from reserve team football on Christmas Eve 1974 for a fee of £170,000. This proved to be money well spent, as the big, bustling centre-forward more than repaid the outlay over the next three seasons.

King George V is introduced to the City players on his visit to Hyde Road on 27 March 1920. A crowd of between 35,000 and 40,000 saw the Blues beat Liverpool 2–1, thanks to two goals from Horace Barnes (News Team International)

Whilst at Maine Road, he regained the England international place he had first won at Everton, and became a key member of a strong Blues' side of the mid 1970s. He was in the teams which beat Newcastle United in the 1976 League Cup final (Royle himself having a goal disallowed), and finished runners-up (by a point) to Liverpool for the League Championship.

After 31 goals in 119 (+2) league and cup appearances for the Blues, Royle joined Bristol City on 15 November 1977. He scored four times on his debut for Bristol City, before a knee injury finished his playing career with Norwich City.

In July 1982, he became the successful and hugely popular manager of Oldham Athletic, where he stayed for over 12 years, before his return to Goodison Park in October 1994.

RUGBY LEAGUE. A total of 13 Rugby League games have been played at Maine Road. The 11 Championship Play Off finals were:

13 May	1934	Salford	8	Castleford	6	att:	69,504
18 May	1946	Wigan	13	Huddersfield	4		67,136
21 June	1947	Wigan	13	Dewsbury	4		40,599
8 May	1948	Warrington	15	Bradford Nor.	5		69,143
14 May	1949	Huddersfield	13	Warrington	12		75,194
13 May	1950	Wigan	20	Huddersfield	2		65,065
12 May	1951	Workington	26	Warrington	11		61,618
9 May	1953	St. Helens	24	Halifax	14		51,083
8 May	1954	Warrington	8	Halifax	7		36,519
14 May	1955	Warrington	7	Oldham	3		49,434
12 May	1956	Hull	10	Halifax	9		36,675

and the two League games were;

18 Jan	1987	Oldham	20	Featherstone	16	2,719
19 Jan	1987	Warrington	24	Barrow	20	2,215

S

SAUNDERS, RON, born Birkenhead, 6 November 1932.
City had three managers during 1973. The first was the
flamboyant Malcolm Allison, the second was the illness-
prone Johnny Hart, and the third was the strict
disciplinarian Ron Saunders.

Saunders had played professional football for 12 years
before turning to management in May 1967. His clubs
included Everton, Gillingham, Watford and Charlton, but
he was most successful, and prolific, at Portsmouth, with
140 goals in 234 league games.

His first taste of management was at Yeovil Town, where
he spent just over a year before a move to Oxford United.
He was with Oxford for only six months when he became
manager of Norwich City in July 1969.

During his time at Carrow Road, Norwich won
promotion to the First Division for the first time in the
club's history, and lost to Tottenham in the 1973 League
Cup Final.

In November 1974, he took over at Maine Road
following the retirement due to ill health, of former Blues'
player Johnny Hart. Undoubtedly a man with a great
knowledge of the game, Saunders' personality and
regimented manner failed to win over the fans, and to a

174

lesser extent, the players. He took the Blues to the 1974 League Cup final, and was also at the helm when Denis Law scored his famous back-heeled goal for City at Old Trafford.

Five months into the job, in April 1975, Saunders was on the move again, this time to Aston Villa, where he stayed for eight years. During his reign at Villa Park, he won both the First Division Championship and the League Cup (Saunders took three different clubs to three consecutive League Cup finals), before resigning in February 1982 and taking over at Birmingham City. At the time of his resignation, Aston Villa were in the quarter-finals of the European Cup, and would go on to win the trophy under the guidance of Saunders' former assistant Tony Barton.

Saunders spent four years with Birmingham City before finishing his football career with West Bromwich Albion in September 1987.

SCANDAL. England's national game was in the news constantly in the mid 1990s for all the wrong reasons. Alleged bribery, players on drugs, drunk driving and fights of various styles and severity provided many a lurid tabloid headline. However, none of this is new. Way back in 1905, Manchester City, unfortunately, were at the centre of one such scandal. The last game of the 1904/05 season saw the Blues away at Aston Villa. City needed to win the game to secure the First Division Championship for the first time in the club's history. A crowd of 20,000 watched the game, which, by all accounts, was not played in friendly circumstances, with fights constantly interrupting the play.

Aston Villa won the game 3–2 (after being 3–0 up), and the Blues finished the season in second place behind Champions Sheffield Wednesday. In the days after the match, rumours began to circulate that money was offered in order to ensure the title would come to Hyde Road.

On 4 August 1905, Billy Meredith was suspended by the FA for allegedly offering Villa's Alec Leake a £10 bribe so that the Blues could win the game. (During the game, Leake had also accused City's Sandy Turnbull of punching him in the mouth.)

175

Meredith immediately denied this accusation but still found himself banned from the game (and the club), until 30 April 1906. Despite being banned from the ground, Meredith turned up regularly (under club orders), to collect his wages. (The FA had stipulated he should receive no wages until the ban was lifted.)

The FA commissioner handling the case, JC Clegg, found out about these wages, ordered the club to cease payments and report Meredith's next visit to the ground. On 14 February 1906, manager Tom E. Maley found himself obliged to report Meredith.

This was the final straw for the man from Chirk. Meredith now changed his story, claiming that he had indeed offered Leake the money. His story went on to say that he was only obeying orders from the manager, who had apparently promised bonuses all round should City clinch the title.

On hearing this new evidence, the FA ordered a full investigation into the club's accounts. A whole manner of irregularities was uncovered, ranging from amateurs being paid, to 'dummy' players on the books, and senior players being paid more than the maximum weekly wage. In the words of American TV drama, the FA 'really threw the book' at City.

The chairman W. Forrest, along with manager Maley and 17 players were banned *sine die*. The club itself was fined £250, and the players, in total, £900.

New manager Harry Newbould inherited this potentially life-threatening situation (of the club anyway) when he took over in June 1906. Nearly 90 years later, thankful as all City fans are, we must surely ask ourselves 'Why did he take the job?'

SCOTLAND – FIRST CITY PLAYER. The first City player to represent Scotland was inside-right George Livingstone. Livingstone, partner on the right to Billy Meredith, played against England in 1906, and would win just one more cap (when he returned north with Rangers).

He scored 20 goals in 88 league and cup games for City before being suspended by the FA in the infamous bribes scandal.

SEAR, CLIFF, born Rhostyllen, 22 September 1936. A tall, long-legged left-back, Cliff Sear was a former miner who joined City as an amateur on 7 June 1955.

At first, he found the travelling from North Wales difficult, but when his amateur side Oswestry Town received £1,750, and he himself was offered a professional contract (on 4 January 1957), Sear realised that the opportunity was too good to miss.

A cultured defender, renowned for his sliding tackle, Sear would go on to make 279 league and cup appearances for the Blues over the next twelve seasons. During that time, he scored just once, in a 4–1 home win over Bolton Wanderers in City's Second Division Championship-winning season of 1965/66. Sear is also the holder of two Welsh Under-23 caps, and one full international cap, won at Wembley in 1963.

On 25 April 1968, he moved to Chester, where he played 49 (+2) league games before going on to the coaching staff.

SECOND DIVISION. Since 1892/93 (its first year), City (or Ardwick), have played 21 seasons in the Second Division.

They have won promotion nine times (see full details under 'PROMOTION' heading), and on six occasions, have won the Second Division Championship. The lowest the Blues have ever finished in this Division was 13th, out of 15, in 1893/94, the club's last season as Ardwick.

SEQUENCE RECORDS
SUCCESSIVE LEAGUE WINS – 9

Win 1 v Tottenham H.	(a)	08.04.12
Win 9 v Bolton W.	(h)	28.09.12

In one season		8
Win 1 v Stoke City	(h)	07.01.05
Win 8 v Blackburn R.	(h)	11.03.05
and		
Win 1 v Plymouth A.	(h)	25.12.46
Win 8 v Swansea T.	(a)	22.02.47

SUCCESSIVE DRAWS IN LEAGUE GAMES – 5

Draw 1 Blackburn R.	(h)	30.12.1899
Draw 5 v Wolves	(a)	03.02.1900

and

Draw 1 v Man. Utd	(a)	19.01.52
Draw 5 v Preston N.E.	(a)	01.03.52

SUCCESSIVE DEFEATS IN LEAGUE GAMES – 6

Defeat 1 v Notts. County	(h)	10.09.10
Defeat 6 v Aston Villa	(a)	15.10.10

and

Defeat 1 v Leeds United	(a)	12.09.56
Defeat 6 v Burnley	(h)	13.10.56

and

Defeat 1 v West Brom	(h)	30.03.59
Defeat 6 v West Ham Utd	(a)	20.04.59

and

Defeat 1 v Bolton W.	(a)	05.11.60
Defeat 6 v Notts. Forest	(h)	17.12.60

and

Defeat 1 v Sheff. Wed	(a)	09.03.63
Defeat 6 v Leicester C.	(a)	06.04.63

RUN OF LEAGUE GAMES WITHOUT A WIN – 17

Last win v Everton	(a)	22.12.79
Next win v Wolves	(a)	12.04.80

If the FA Cup defeat at Halifax is included, this run is extended to 18 games.

The worst overall spell was from a win at home v Derby County on 05.01.52, up to a home win v Charlton Athletic on 15.11.52.

In this spell City won two league games out of a possible 31. Both were at Maine Road, v Liverpool 14.04.52, and v Manchester United on 30.08.52.

RUN OF LEAGUE GAMES WITHOUT A DRAW – 20

Last draw v Burton Swifts	(h)	26.11.1892
Next draw v Notts. County	(h)	28.10.1893

In one season   18
Last draw v Barnsley   (h)   01.10.26
Next draw v Notts. Forest   (h)   19.02.27

RUN OF LEAGUE GAMES WITHOUT A DEFEAT – 22
Last defeat v Grimsby Town   (a)   25.12.36
Next defeat v Wolves   (a)   28.08.37
and
Last defeat v Birmingham C.   (a)   09.11.46
Next defeat v Newcastle Utd.   (h)   03.05.47

SHERON, MIKE, born Liverpool, 11 January 1972. Yet another product of City's youth policy, striker Mike Sheron was playing for Warrington side Penlake Juniors when he signed schoolboy forms in 1986.

On 2 July 1990, he turned professional, and his debut came as a substitute in a 1–0 home defeat by Everton on 17 September the following year.

A player with good positional sense, Sheron formed a good understanding with Niall Quinn which produced 19 league goals in their first season together. The holder of 13 England Under 21 caps, Sheron played with (and roomed with) Garry Flitcroft on international duty, continuing a playing partnership begun as thirteen-year-olds.

The arrival of Paul Walsh and Uwe Rösler put Sheron's first team place in jeopardy and on 26 August 1994, after 98 (+22) appearances and 28 goals, he moved to Norwich City for £1 million.

SHIPS. In 1894 the Manchester Ship Canal was opened and, although not immediately, Manchester was to become a major port of call for ships from the four corners of the world.

Four years later Manchester Liners Ltd, based on the canal, came into existence. Over the next 90 years almost one new ship a year came into use, each one carrying Manchester in the name.

The third such ship (back in 1898) was the *Manchester City* (the first of four ships named after the club), and was the first built specially for Manchester Liners. (The previous two had been bought and renamed.)

At 461 feet long and weighing 7696 tonnes, she was the largest meat ship of the time, and she proved a great boost to the canal, whose doubters didn't think it could handle such a size. Initially transporting meat from Canada, the first *Manchester City* began trafficking frozen meat from the Argentine in 1906. It continued on this route until being broken up in Norway in 1929.

The second *Manchester City* (weighing 7296 tonnes), was built in 1937 to celebrate City's Championship success. In 1939 she was requisitioned by the Royal Navy and spent the early years of the war as a mine-layer. In 1941 she was transferred (as an auxiliary ship) to the East Indies, before returning to Manchester Liners in March 1946.

The third *Manchester City* (and largest at 8734 tonnes) was built in 1964, and served for seven years before being sold off. The fourth and last *Manchester City* (3598 tonnes) was built in 1978. She too saw service for seven years before being sold for charter in 1985.

SIMPSON, FITZROY, born Trowbridge, 26 February 1970. A tough-tackling left-sided midfield player, Fitzroy Simpson began his playing career with Swindon Town as a trainee in 1986. He turned professional in 1988 and, after working his way through the ranks, became a key player in a Swindon side that won the First Division play-off place, only to be denied by the FA's investigation into irregular financial dealings. On 3 March 1992, after 98 (+32) league and cup games for Swindon, manager Peter Reid acquired Simpson's services for £550,000. His debut came as a substitute four days later as the Blues crashed 4–0 at Queen's Park Rangers.

Since that debut, Simpson has been a regular member of the first team squad, but he has been unable to hold down a permanent spot. Initially kept out by seasoned campaigner Steve McMahon, Simpson then found it difficult to oust youngsters Garry Flitcroft and Steve Lomas. In order to maintain match fitness, he spent a month on loan with Bristol City during the 1994/95 season.

SIMPSON, PAUL, born Carlisle, 26 July 1966. A former Carlisle and Cumbria Boy, Paul Simpson signed apprentice forms for the Blues on 26 July 1982, his 16th birthday. (Professional forms on 1 August 1983.)

The abilities of this skilful left winger gained him a regular reserve team spot, and when he made his first team debut against Coventry City at Maine Road on 2 October 1983, he was still only 16.

Despite this early promise, it wasn't until the end of the 1984/85 season that he established a regular senior place. He scored eight times in 30 (+7) league games in the 1985/86 campaign, including three in seven days in August.

On 31 October 1988, Simpson moved to Oxford United, where he played 138 (+6) league games before being sold to Derby County in February 1992. Whilst at Maine Road he scored 24 goals in 127 (+28) league and cup appearances.

SMALLEST PLAYER. According to existing records the smallest player ever to appear for City was winger Harry Anders.

Anders stood just 5 feet 2 inches tall and played for the Blues from 1953 to 1956. Other players around the 5 feet 4 inches mark were Fred Fayers, Garry Buckley, Herbert Burgess, Ronnie Hildersley and James Hope.

SMITH, GEORGE, born Fleetwood, 7 February 1921. George Smith joined City in the 1938 close season, but his career at Maine Road didn't actually commence for real until after World War Two.

He made nearly 100 wartime appearances for the Blues and also guested for Hearts and Burnley. It was whilst serving his country in South Africa that he sustained a gunshot wound which resulted in his having a hand partially amputated.

He eventually made his league debut on 31 August 1946, and before long became well known for jabbing his 'stump' into opposing defenders as he battled for possession. He would prove a prolific scorer for the club, netting 78 goals in 175 league and cup appearances – including all five in a 5–1 victory over Newport County on 14 June 1947.

He moved to Chesterfield on 18 October 1951, where he played 250 league games before spells with several non-league sides in the Manchester area.

SMITH, WALTER, born Leicester, 25 March 1884. Walter Smith joined City from his hometown club Leicester Fosse on 4 July 1906 to replace Jack Hillman in the wake of the scandal that had rocked the club that year.

It was an astute piece of business by manager Harry Newbould as Smith quickly proved himself a worthy member of the City 'Great Goalkeepers Union' despite standing just 5 feet 9 inches. Although he lost his place to John Lyall during the promotion winning season of 1909/10, it was a minor blemish on a City career that spanned 14 years. He played 256 league and cup games for the Blues in a career that went on briefly after World War One.

He moved to Port Vale on 19 October 1920, but made only 42 appearances in three years before retiring.

SPONSORS. Since the introduction of sponsorship at the beginning of the 1982/83 season City have had just three major sponsors.

These are:

	1982/83	SAAB
	1983/84	SAAB
	1984/85	SAAB
	1985/86	PHILIPS
	1986/87	PHILIPS
	1987/88	PHILIPS
from	1988/89	BROTHER

SPROTSON, BERT, born Sandbach, 22 June 1915. An outstanding right-back, Bert Sprotson became an England international shortly after his 21st birthday while at Leeds United, and was valued at £9,500 when he was transferred to Tottenham Hotspur in June 1938.

Sprotson couldn't settle in London and four months later was involved in a strange £10,000 move to Maine Road. He travelled north with his Spurs colleagues on Friday 4 November for a league match, signed for City after hectic negotiations, and made his debut against his former team-mates the following day. (City won the match 2–0.)

War broke out soon afterwards and robbed Sprotson and City of the best years of his career. He played over 80 times for the Blues during the war, but when the 1946/47 season arrived, he had become a near veteran of 31.

He played on to record 131 league and cup appearances and win a Second Division Championship medal before a move to Ashton National. He later became a physiotherapist with Bolton Wanderers.

SPURDLE, BILLY, born Guernsey, 28 January 1926. Billy Spurdle became the first Channel Islander to appear in an FA Cup final when he played at Wembley for City against Newcastle United in 1955.

Evacuated to the mainland in 1940, just hours before the German occupation, Spurdle stayed on after the war and began his professional career with Oldham Athletic. It was from Boundary Park that he joined City on 21 January 1950. At Maine Road he developed into a useful all-round player, appearing at wing-half, inside-forward and as a winger, scoring 33 goals in 172 league and cup games before being transferred to Port Vale on 23 November 1956.

He was unlucky earlier that year not to have played in his second successive Cup Final, when boils ruled him out of the City team that beat Birmingham City.

STEPANOVIC, DRAGOSLAV, born Rekovac, Yugoslavia, 30 August 1948. The opening game of the 1979/80 season saw the Blues give league debuts to four players. These were the homegrown Tommy Caton, and signings Michael Robinson and Steve MacKenzie.

The fourth player was defender Dragoslav Stepanovic, a £140,000 signing from Bundesliga side Wormatia Worms on 14 August.

Stepanovic was a vastly experienced international who had played 44 games for Yugoslavia at the time of his arrival at Maine Road.

Unaccustomed to the speed of the game in England (a difficulty not exclusively his), Stepanovic made 13 (+1) appearances in his first season with Manchester City. The following season he played in just one senior game (the second, a 4–0 home defeat by Sunderland), before becoming a regular fixture in the reserve side.

In July 1981, manager John Bond allowed Stepanovic to return to Wormatia Worms where he would eventually become coach.

STEWART, PAUL, born Manchester, 7 October 1964. Paul Stewart began his playing career with Fourth Division Blackpool when he joined them on apprentice forms in April 1981. In February the following year he made his league debut (albeit as a substitute), and his powerful forward play would quickly establish him in the first team.

On 19 March 1987, after 56 goals in 188 (+13) league games for the Seasiders, Stewart arrived at Maine Road for a fee of £200,000. His two goals in 11 games for the Blues that season could not prevent relegation, although he more than proved himself the following season.

In 1987/88 he scored 24 times in 40 league games, including a hat-trick in the 10–1 demolition of Huddersfield Town, to make him City's top scorer.

In the summer of 1988, City (not for the first time in their history), were experiencing financial limitations. On 12 June these problems were somewhat alleviated when Stewart moved to Tottenham Hotspur for £1,700,000. (To date, this is City's record transfer fee received.)

He maintained his goalscoring prowess forged at Blackpool with 30 goals in 63 league and cup games in City's colours.

Stewart spent nearly four years at White Hart Lane, where he won an FA Cup medal and three England caps. In July 1992 he became a £2,300,000 Liverpool player, and was converted from a striker to a midfielder.

STREET NAMES. In 1977 Manchester City Council named a number of Moss Side streets after great City players of the past.

These streets (all closes) bear the names of: Horace Barnes, Eric Brook, Tommy Browell, Sammy Cookson, Sam Cowan, Billy Meredith, Fred Tilson, and three walks are named after Frank Swift, Jimmy McMullan and the gentleman Max Woosnam.

All these streets are located just minutes from the ground in an area off Claremont Road.

SUBSTITUTE – FIRST. The first named league substitute for City was Glyn Pardoe for the opening game of the 1965/66 season. The match took place on 21 August at Ayresome Park, Middlesbrough and finished goalless.

City's first used substitute in the league was Roy Cheetham at Wolves on 30 August 1965. He came on as a replacement for Mike Summerbee in a game City won 4–2.

SUMMERBEE, MIKE, born Cheltenham, 15 December 1942. Without doubt one of City's greatest players of all time, Mike Summerbee is arguably the most popular ever to wear the sky blue shirt.

His performances for amateur side Cheltenham Town brought him to the attention of Swindon Town, where, as a 16-year-old, he made his league debut in 1959. He scored 39 goals in 218 league games for Swindon, and helped them win promotion to the Second Division in 1963. On 16 January 1965 Summerbee played (and scored) at Maine Road, as Swindon beat City 2–1 in front of just 8,015 people, City's lowest attendance ever for a league match.

When Joe Mercer and Malcolm Allison began rebuilding City in the summer of 1965, the name Summerbee came to the forefront of requirements. (Mercer had played wartime football with Mike's father George, and had kept a close eye on the blossoming career of Summerbee junior.)

On 20 August he arrived at Maine Road, for what turned out to be the amazing bargain price of £35,000. Despite contrary accounts, Summerbee was not Mercer's first signing for the Blues. This honour fell to Scottish winger Ralph Brand who had signed on 11 August. The 1965/66 season saw a revitalised City win the Second Division Championship. Summerbee made his debut in the opening game (a 1–1 draw at Middlesbrough), and played in all 42 league games, scoring eight times.

Over the next five years City were without question the country's top side, winning trophies almost at will. Summerbee's contribution to these efforts is immeasurable.

185

Mike Summerbee scores City's first goal in the 1967/68 Championship decider at Newcastle. Neil Young (2) and Francis Lee shared the goals in the Blues' 4–3 win (News Team International)

As part of a magnificent five-man forward line, his strong, fearless wing play provided countless opportunities for the likes of Lee, Bell and Young. (Let us not forget also, that he did himself score on occasion, not least in the Championship decider at Newcastle.)

England manager Sir Alf Ramsey rewarded these performances by awarding Summerbee the first of his eight caps in a 1–1 draw at Hampden Park on 24 February 1968. (He scored just once for England – in a 1–1 Wembley draw against Switzerland on 10 November 1971.)

Perhaps the biggest disappointment of his Maine Road career was when injury forced him to miss the 1970 European Cup Winners' Cup Final against Gornik in Vienna.

During the glory days Summerbee had become a boutique owner, and would later establish a successful shirt making business.

On 13 July 1975, after 67 goals in 441 (+2) league and cup games (placing him eighth overall), Mike Summerbee moved to Burnley for £25,000. He later played for Blackpool and Stockport County, where he had a spell as player/manager.

Thirty years after arriving at Maine Road, the name of Summerbee is still associated with Manchester City. Mike is currently the club's sales manager, whilst son Nicky is flying along the same wings as his father in the Blues' first team.

SUMMERBEE, NICKY, born Altrincham, 26 August 1971. When Nicky Summerbee came on as substitute for Swindon Town against Wolves on 3 September 1989 he became the third-generation Summerbee to play league football.

His grandfather George played nearly 150 league games either side of World War Two for Aldershot, Preston, Chester and finally Barrow. His father Mike of course was a member of the great City sides of the late 60s and early 70s and needs no introduction to Blues followers.

Initially signed by Swindon as a trainee in October 1987, Summerbee played 112 league games for the west country side before a £1.5 million move to City on 22 June 1994. In Swindon's colours he had an outstanding game at Maine Road in February 1994, and following the Robins' relegation, manager Brian Horton had no hesitation in obtaining his signature.

His debut came in the opening game of the 1994/95 season (a 3–0 defeat at Highbury) and he scored his first goal for the Blues in a 4–1 Coca-Cola League Cup victory against Barnet on 5 October. The subject of obvious comparison with his famous father, Nicky played right-wing and midfield when he first arrived, but midway through the season injuries forced him to move to right-back and it was in this position that he gave perhaps his best performances.

The holder of three England Under-21 caps looks certain to become a regular at Maine Road for many years to come.

SWIFT, FRANK, born Blackpool, 26 December 1913. At six feet 2 inches tall and weighing around 14 stones, with hands like 'frying pans', Frank Swift was one of the best goalkeepers the world has ever seen.

'Big Swifty' began his career with Blackpool Gas Works before moving along the Fylde coast to Fleetwood. It was from here that he signed for City on 21 October 1932 as an amateur, turning professional on 16 November. He made his first team debut on Christmas Day 1933 in a 3–1 win at Derby County, and played in 22 league games that season. Over the next four seasons Swift played in every single league game (42 per season), and missed just one in 1938/39. During this time he won a First Division Championship medal and an FA Cup Winner's medal, even though he did faint after the final whistle against Portsmouth.

When war broke out Swift became a special constable, but gave up traffic control on the first day. The volume of traffic forced the confused Swift to say, 'Now I know how full-backs feel when playing against Stanley Matthews'.

During the war he played 153 times for City and 14 times (inc. victory internationals) for England. The first of his 19 non-wartime caps came on 28 September 1946, when he played in the 7–2 triumph over Northern Ireland in Belfast. On 16 May the following year, Swift captained the national side (England beating Italy 4–0 in Turin), thereby becoming the first goalkeeper ever to do so.

In September 1949 after 369 league and cup appearances for City, Swift retired from the game. His place in the first team was eventually taken by another great goalkeeper, Bert Trautmann.

Frank Swift later became a respected sports journalist, and was to be one of the many killed in the tragic Munich aircrash of February 1958, after he had covered Manchester United's European game in Belgrade.

T

TALLEST PLAYER. From the records that exist, the tallest City player was Joe Corrigan at 6 feet 4½ inches. Another goalkeeper, John Savage, was 6 feet 4 inches, while four other players are recorded as being 6 feet 3 inches: goalkeepers Albert Gray and James Nichols, defender Michel Vonk, and striker Niall Quinn.

TELEVISION – FIRST GAME. When Bert Trautmann broke his neck against Birmingham City in the 1956 FA Cup final, it would be six months before he returned to first team action.

On 15 December 1956, a crowd of 30,329 saw a Wolves side beat Trautmann's City 3–2 at Maine Road. The game was shown on BBC TV's *Sports Special* that same evening, and was the first time a game at Maine Road had been televised.

TEXACO CUP. Another tournament of early season 'competitive friendlies', City have appeared in five Texaco Cup matches.

These are:

15 Sept   1971   Round One   v Airdrieonians   (h)   2–2   att: 15,033
                                          (Mellor, Doyle)

189

27 Sept	1971	Round One	v Airdrieonians	(a)	0–2	att: 13,700
3 Aug	1974	Group One	v Blackpool	(a)	1–1	att: 12,342
			(Tueart)			
6 Aug	1974	Group One	v Sheffield Utd	(a)	2–4	att: 9,358
			(Summerbee, Law)			
10 Aug	1974	Group One	v Oldham Ath	(h)	2–1	att: 13,880
			(Lee, Tueart)			

City failed to qualify for the later stages.

THOMSON, JOCK, born Thornton, Fifeshire, 6 July 1906. John Ross Thomson spent nearly 14 years as a wing-half with Everton prior to World War Two.

As a member of that great Merseyside team of the era, he won First and Second Division Championship medals as well as an FA Cup Winners' medal. The holder of just one Scottish cap, Thomson would eventually lose his place in the Everton side to another future City manager, Joe Mercer.

When Sam Cowan left City in the summer of 1947, the club waited for four months before the arrival of new manager Thomson in November. His first full season in charge, 1948/49, saw City finish seventh in Division One, although they scored only 47 times in the whole 42 match season. The following season was much worse. City managed just 36 goals (and eight wins) in the league and were relegated.

Jock Thomson's less than memorable two and a half years as City's manager ended when he resigned in April 1950. He never managed another club, opting instead to become a pub landlord in Carnoustie. He ran the pub until 1974, five years before his death.

THORNLEY, IRVINE, born Hayfield, 1883. There were few more popular players among City followers in the early part of the century than former butcher Irvine Thornley.

The supporters recognised his tireless spirit and wholehearted efforts by making him the first player to receive £1,000 for his benefit – a huge amount at the time.

Thornley joined City from Glossop North End on 7 April 1904 for a reported £450 and made his debut two days later in a 2–1 home defeat by West Bromwich Albion. He went on to score 93 goals for the club in 203 league and cup appearances.

Thornley, however, was quite a firebrand, and was involved in a number of controversial incidents during his career, and was once suspended for a whole year.

His talents earned him an England cap against Wales in 1907, and he also represented the Football League. He won a Second Division Championship medal in 1909/10 (when he was one of three players who scored 12 goals), before moving to South Shields on 12 August 1912.

TILSON, FRED, born Barnsley, 19 April 1903. Freddie Tilson was one of five players signed by City in a quest for promotion in 1927/28, and overcame serious injury problems to become an integral part of the successful Blues' sides of the 1930s.

Tilson signed for City along with Barnsley team-mate Eric Brook in a joint deal that cost the club £6,000 on 14 March 1928, but a bad injury sustained at Old Trafford the following season, then a lengthy illness, put a damper on his progress. He eventually regained full fitness and with it a regular place in a blossoming City side for whom he quickly became the leading goalscorer.

Tilson's bad luck surfaced again, however, when he was injured in a league match just prior to the 1933 FA Cup final against Everton, and was left out much to the disappointment of his colleagues. City lost that final 3–0, but they – and Tilson – more than made up for it the following year.

The Blues won through to Wembley again, with Tilson scoring four times in a remarkable 6–1 semi-final victory against Aston Villa at Huddersfield, then hitting both goals against Portsmouth in the final.

That summer he was capped for England, where he scored six times in just four internationals.

In 1936/37 Freddie Tilson climaxed his City career by winning a League Championship medal before moving to Northampton Town on 11 March 1938 with 274 league and cup games and 132 goals under his belt.

In later years he returned to his beloved Maine Road to serve the club as coach, assistant manager and chief scout. The man whose goals place him joint eighth top scorer for City died in November 1972, aged 69.

TOLMIE, JIM, born Glasgow, 20 November 1960. Scottish Under-21 international Jim Tolmie began his professional career with Greenock Morton in 1978.

By May 1983 he found himself struggling to maintain a regular first team place with Belgian side FC Lokeren. On 25 July that year new manager Billy McNeill revived his career when he signed him for City.

His debut came in the opening game of the 1983/84 season (a 2–0 win at Crystal Palace), and Tolmie found the net six times in his first eight outings.

He played in all bar one of the 42 league games that term, scoring 13 times, as the Blues missed out on promotion by one place. The following season proved better for City but not for Tolmie. The Blues won promotion but Tolmie's appearances were limited to 17, ten of which were as substitute.

In March 1986 he moved to Carlisle United on loan before a permanent move to Scandinavia in the close season. Tolmie scored 19 goals in 50 (+17) league and cup games for City.

TOSELAND, ERNIE, born Kettering, 17 March 1905. Ernie Toseland was a former rugby three-quarter whose tremendous speed earned him the reputation of being one of the best right wingers of the 1930s.

He was also one of the unluckiest as he was never to win an England cap at a time when there was a glut of outstanding wingers in the game, although he did represent the Football League on one occasion.

Toseland joined City on 1 March 1929 from Coventry City, for whom he had made a dramatic impact with 11 goals in 22 appearances. Following his debut against Bury on 20 April, he quickly became a fixture in a City team which lost and won consecutive FA Cup Finals, and then went on to take the League Championship in 1936/37. His contribution to that golden era earned him a substantial £650 benefit from the grateful Board of Directors.

192

After ten years at Maine Road with 409 league and cup appearances and 76 goals, Toseland moved to Sheffield Wednesday on 15 March 1939, but later guested for City in two wartime games.

Toseland was still to be found playing, as enthusiastically as ever, in the Cheshire County League in 1945/46. He died in October 1987, aged 82.

TOWERS, TONY, born Manchester, 13 April 1952. A vastly underrated player during his time at Maine Road, Tony Towers later earned international recognition after a move to Sunderland on 11 March 1974. (Towers was part of a deal which brought Dennis Tueart and Mick Horswill to Maine Road.)

Moston-born Towers, a former Manchester Boys player, was a skilful, industrious midfield worker who was fortunate enough to learn his trade under the guidance of Joe Mercer and Malcolm Allison at a time when City were winning everything in sight.

He made his first team debut at Southampton the week before the 1969 FA Cup final, and was brought along gradually not establishing a regular spot until the 1970/71 season.

Towers packed an explosive shot and played in the City side that won the 1970 European Cup Winners' Cup final against Gornik in Vienna. Perhaps his most famous moment at Maine Road came in the quarter-final of that competition, when his stunning long-range drive in extra time decided a tricky tie against Portuguese side Academica de Coimbra.

He won England Under-23 honours at City and clocked up 150 (+8) league and cup appearances with 12 goals, before his transfer to Sunderland saw him progress to the full national side.

He won three full caps and later played for Birmingham City, Rochdale and NASL side Tacoma amongst others.

TRANSFER RECORDS – TOP 10

	Player	From	Date	Amount
1	Keith Curle	Wimbledon	06.08.91	£2,500,000
2	Terry Phelan	Wimbledon	24.08.92	2,500,000

3	Georgiou Kinkladze	Dynamo Tblisi	14.07.95	2,000,000
4	Alan Kernaghan	Middlesbrough	17.09.93	1,600,000
5	Nicky Summerbee	Swindon Town	22.06.94	1,500,000
6	Steve Daley	Wolves	05.09.79	1,437,500
7	Kevin Reeves	Norwich City	11.03.80	1,200,000
7	Trevor Francis	Notts Forest	03.09.81	1,200,000
9	Peter Beagrie	Everton	24.03.94	1,100,000
9	Clive Allen	Bordeaux	14.08.89	1,100,000

The record transfer fee received by City is £1,700,000 when Paul Stewart moved to Tottenham on 12 June 1988.

TRAUTMANN, BERT, born Bremen, Germany, 22 October 1923. When the great Frank Swift retired in 1949, City took the brave and controversial decision to sign Bernhard Carl Trautmann, an ex-German paratrooper who had been a prisoner of war.

The war was still fresh in many Mancunian's minds, and hostile letters and protests were hurled at the club following his signature.

Manager Jock Thomson, along with the full support of the rest of his players, helped Trautmann overcome these early difficulties to become one of City's greatest and most popular players of all time.

After his capture in Normandy, Trautmann was sent to a prisoner of war camp in Ashton-in-Makerfield. When the war was over, he played for St. Helens Town, and it was from here that he signed for the Blues, originally as an amateur on 7 October 1949. Less than a month later he had turned professional.

His debut on 19 November 1949 came on the wrong side of a 3–0 scoreline at Bolton, and he would play 26 league games in his debut season. Over the next six seasons, Trautmann's tremendous physical strength saw him miss just five of a possible 252 league games. He played in both of City's mid-1950s FA Cup finals, and will be forever remembered for carrying on playing despite a broken neck in the 1956 triumph over Birmingham City. His heroics in that game won him the Footballer of the Year trophy.

When he retired on 10 May 1964, Bert Trautmann had played in 545 league and cup games for City (placing him fourth overall), and had also been responsible for the introduction of the European style low-cut soccer boot to England. His abilities and overall manner had so won over the City fans that nearly 48,000 turned out for his testimonial in 1964.

It is tragic that Trautmann's only international honours came as a Football League representative against the Irish League and the Italian League in 1960. Politics prevented one of the greatest goalkeepers the world has ever seen from playing for his native Germany.

After Maine Road Trautmann became manager of Stockport County, Wellington Town and the Burmese national team. He spent many years coaching all over the world before finally settling down and sharing his time between Spain and Germany. Even today, despite being over 70, the amazingly fit-looking Bert Trautmann looks more than capable of still being able to play in goal.

TUEART, DENNIS, born Newcastle, 27 November 1949. When Dennis Tueart scored his spectacular winning goal in the 1976 League Cup final he must have had mixed feelings. He had just scored one of the best goals ever seen at Wembley against Newcastle United, the team he had supported as a boy.

A former Newcastle Boys player, Tueart began his career as a teenager with Sunderland in August 1967. Seven years later he was a Wembley winner with the Second Division Wearsiders as they beat the mighty Leeds United in the 1973 FA Cup final.

On 11 March 1974, Tueart, along with teammate Mick Horswill, arrived at Maine Road in an exchange deal involving City's Tony Towers. His debut (and Horswill's) came two days later in a goalless Maine Road derby. A fast, direct winger, Tueart quickly established himself as a fans' favourite who became City's regular penalty taker. Only Francis Lee and Eric Brook have scored more penalties for the club.

The lure of the NASL beckoned on 13 February 1978, and Tueart moved to the New York Cosmos for £250,000.

Dennis Tueart – the scorer of one of the most spectacular goals ever seen at Wembley (News Team International)

He stayed in the United States for nearly 2 years before returning to Maine Road on 31 January 1980. His second league debut for City was also goalless. This was against Norwich City on 1 March, indeed it was to be four games before City, and Tueart, scored again. On 9 July 1983, Dennis Tueart moved to Stoke City, before finishing his league playing career with Burnley. In both spells with City, he played a total of 258 (+10) league and cup games and scored 108 goals.

TURNBULL, ALEX, born Hurlford, 1884. Inside-forward Alex 'Sandy' Turnbull scored 60 goals in 119 league and cup games for City in the early part of the century. He arrived at Hyde Road on 27 July 1902, but had to wait four months, until 15 November, for his league debut. This came in a 3–2 defeat at Bristol City. By the end of that season, Turnbull was the owner of a Second Division Championship medal and City were back in the top flight. He scored 5 of City's amazing 35 goals in a six-match run in January and February 1903. During this same period, the Blues conceded just three. Turnbull was a member of the City sides that won the FA Cup and finished second and third in the First Division, and his 19 goal tally in the 1904/05 league campaign made him the club's top scorer for the season.

Following the infamous 1906 illegal payments scandal, Turnbull was one of four City players transferred to Manchester United, where he won his second FA Cup medal.

When war came, he joined the Manchester Regiment, and was tragically killed at Arras on 3 May 1917.

U

UEFA CUP. To date, City have played 14 games in this competition, designed to compensate European sides who have narrowly missed out on either league or cup success. These games are:

Round One	1st leg	13 Sept 1972 (Mellor, Marsh)	2–2	v Valencia att. 21,698	(h)
Round One	2nd leg	27 Sept 1972 (Marsh)	1–2	v Valencia att. 35,000	(a)
Round One	1st leg	15 Sept 1976 (Kidd)	1–0	v Juventus att. 36,955	(h)
Round One	2nd leg	29 Sept 1976	0–2	v Juventus att. 55,000	(a)
Round One	1st leg	14 Sept 1977 (Barnes, Channon)	2–2	v Widzew Lodz att. 33,695	(h)
Round One	2nd leg	28 Sept 1977	0–0	v Widzew Lodz att. 40,000	(a)
Round One	1st leg	13 Sept 1978 (Watson)	1–1	v FC Twente att. 12,000	(a)
Round One	2nd leg	27 Sept 1978 (Kidd, Bell, opp og.)	3–2	v FC Twente (h) att. 29,330	
Round Two	1st leg	18 Oct 1978 (Kidd 2, Palmer, Hartford)	4–0	v Standard Liege att. 27,489	(h)

Round Two	2nd leg	01 Nov 1978	0–2	v Standard Liege att. 25,000	(a)
Round Three	1st leg	23 Nov 1978 (Power, Kidd)	2–2	v AC Milan att. 40,000	(a)
Round Three	2nd leg	06 Dec 1978 (Kidd, Booth, Hartford)	3–0	v AC Milan att. 38,026	(h)
Round Four	1st leg	07 Mar 1979 (Channon)	1–1	v Borussia Monchengladbach att. 39,005	(h)
Round Four	2nd leg	20 Mar 1979 (Deyna)	1–3	v Borussia Monchengladbach att. 30,000	(a)

UMBRO. When Blues' skipper Sam Cowan raised the FA Cup at Wembley in 1934, he, like all of his team-mates, was wearing an Umbro shirt. City were the first professional club ever to wear the Umbro shirt, and they have been associated with the former Wilmslow-based company ever since. 61 years later, after League, Cup and European successes, City are still wearing Umbro's products, continuing one of the longest links between any sponsor in sport.

The company started in 1922 (as Humphrey Brothers), and was incorporated two years later under the trading name Umbro International. In those early days ladies continued working at home after finishing a day's work. On a good night, one lady could produce 12 shirts. Harold Humphreys kept his entire stock (sometimes up to £10 in value), in his mother's cupboard. Humble beginnings for today's multi-national company, whose famous double diamond can now be seen worn by clubs such as Inter Milan, Celtic and Ajax, as well as four of the five Home Countries and world champions Brazil.

UNITED STATES – CITY PLAYERS IN. When researching this book, it came as a surprise that so many City players had actually played in the United States.

The following is a list of American clubs with which Manchester City players have been associated. Some of them are indoor soccer sides, and not all the outdoor ones were members of the NASL. Canadian clubs who were members of the NASL are included.

Where no team name is given, I was unable to trace precise information.

BARNES, PETER (Tampa Bay Rowdies), BELL, COLIN (San Jose Earthquake), BENNETT, DAVID (Portland Timbers), BLAIR, TOM (Fall River, New Brighton), BOND, KEVIN (Seattle Sounders), CALVEY, MITCHELL (Baltimore Orioles), CHEETHAM, ROY (Detroit Cougars), CONWAY, JIM (Portland Timbers), CORRIGAN, JOE (Seattle Sounders), CROSS, DAVID (Vancouver Whitecaps), DALEY, STEVE (Seattle Sounders, San Diego Sockers), DAVIDSON, DUNCAN (Tulsa Roughnecks), DAVIES, IAN (Detroit Express), DEYNA, KAZIU (San Diego Sockers), DONACHIE, WILLIE (Portland Timbers), FASHANU, JUSTIN (Los Angeles Heat), FERGUSON, ARCHIE (Baltimore Orioles), FRANCIS, TREVOR (Detroit Express), FUTCHER, RON (Minnesota Kicks, Portland Timbers, Tulsa Roughnecks), GILLESPIE, BILLY (not known), HAMILL, MICKEY (Fall River Marksmen), HAMMOND, GEOFF (Connecticut Bicentennials), HARTFORD, ASA (Fort Lauderdale Sun), HORNE, STAN (Denver Dynamo), HUTCHISON, TOMMY (Seattle Sounders), HYNDS, TOM (not known), JOHNSON, DAVID (Tulsa Roughnecks), KIDD, BRIAN (Atlanta Chiefs, Fort Lauderdale Strikers, Minnesota Kicks), KINSEY, STEVE (Minnesota Kicks, Tacoma, Los Angeles, Fort Lauderdale), LEE, STUART (Portland Timbers, Tampa Bay Rowdies, Los Angeles Lazers, St. Louis Steamboats), LESTER, MIKE (Washington Diplomats), LITTLE, TOM (Baltimore Orioles), MACRAE, KEITH (Philadelphia Fury, Portland Timbers), MARSH, RODNEY (Tampa Bay Rowdies), McALINDEN, BOBBY (Los Angeles Aztecs, Memphis Rogues), PARK, TERRY (Fort Lauderdale Strikers, Minnesota Kicks), REID, NICKY (Seattle Sounders), RYAN, JOHN (Seattle Sounders), SUGRUE, PAUL (Kansas City Comets), TOWERS, TONY (Tampa Bay Rowdies, Tacoma, Montreal Manic, Vancouver Whitecaps),

TUEART, DENNIS (New York Cosmos), WALLACE, ALEX (Baltimore Orioles), WALSH, MIKE (Fort Lauderdale Strikers), WATSON, DAVE (Fort Lauderdale Sun, Vancouver Whitecaps), WHELAN, TONY (Fort Lauderdale Strikers), WOOSNAM, PHIL (Atlanta Chiefs).

V

VICTORIES IN A SEASON – LEAST. The fewest victories recorded by City in a single league season is eight. This has happened three times, in 1893/94 from 28 games, 1949/50 from 42 and 1986/87 also from 42.

The last two seasons saw City relegated to the Second Division. Ardwick (in their final season) finished 13th (from 15) in 1893/94.

VICTORIES IN A SEASON – MOST. The most victories recorded in a single league season is 26, from 42 league games, in 1946/47.

The Blues won the Second Division Championship that season, and scored 78 goals. The top scorer was George Smith with 23.

VICTORY INTERNATIONALS. Players who played in Victory Internationals while on City's books were:

World War One – Horace Barnes
                Edwin Hughes
                George Wynn
World War Two – Peter Doherty
                Frank Swift

Doherty played just once while with City, and another after he was transferred to Derby County. Frank Swift played in four, along with ten wartime internationals.

At the end of World War One, Billy Meredith played in one game. He was officially a Manchester United player at the time, but had been on loan to City when picked.

VILJOEN, COLIN, born Johannesburg, 20 June 1948. Midfielder Colin Viljoen had played over 300 league games in 11 years at Ipswich when he signed for City on 15 August 1978. A naturalised Briton, he had been a member of Bobby Robson's fine Ipswich sides of the mid to late 70s, although injury caused him eventually to lose his first team spot.

His debut for the Blues came on 16 September 1978 in a 4–1 away win at Chelsea, thanks largely to a Ron Futcher hat-trick, and the £100,000 player played 16 league games that season. On 13 March 1980 manager Malcolm Allison sold Viljoen to Chelsea. He played in just 35 (+3) league and cup games for City, but failed to find the net once.

VONK, MICHEL, born Alkmaar, Holland, 28 October 1968. At 6 feet 3 inches tall, central defender Michel Vonk is one of the tallest players ever to play for City. A £500,000 signing from Dutch side SVV Dordrecht on 7 March 1992, Vonk provided height and stability to City's defence and formed a solid partnership with captain Keith Curle.

He made his debut for City as a substitute on 21 March in a game the Blues lost 2–0 at Nottingham Forest. An ankle injury sustained against Middlesbrough in September 1992 kept him out for four months, but on his return, he scored the winning goal in a 4th round FA Cup tie at Queen's Park Rangers.

The return to form of Alan Kernaghan in the 1994/95 season saw Vonk's first team chances restricted. Although a situation not completely satisfactory for Vonk, it made a refreshing change for manager Brian Horton to have players of the experience and ability of the Dutchman fit and ready, and part of the first team squad.

W

WAGSTAFFE, DAVID, born Manchester, 5 April 1943. The 1960/61 season saw City's number 11 shirt worn by the experienced Clive Colbridge, and the 17-year-old David Wagstaffe.

Having signed professional forms on 16 May 1960, 'Waggy' had progressed through the junior ranks at Maine Road, and made his first team debut in a 1–1 home draw with Sheffield Wednesday on 7 September 1960. By the end of that season, he had scored three times in 22 league games, and his direct wing play and crosses had made him a favourite with the City faithful.

An ever-present in the league the following season, the former England Youth and Football League representative would make 161 league and cup appearances (with eight goals), before a £44,750 move to Wolves on Boxing Day 1964. In his last four games for City, the Blues had scored 20 goals, and his transfer coincided with the switching on of the ground's new floodlights.

He made 324 league appearances for Wolves in just over 11 years (as well as playing for Wolves against City in the 1974 League Cup final), before returning north to Blackburn and later Blackpool.

WALES – FIRST CITY PLAYER. The first Blues' player to represent Wales was Joe Davies, a forward who had two spells with the club in the 1890s. He won three of his 11 caps whilst at Hyde Road. The first two (as an Ardwick player), were against England and Scotland in 1891, and his third (as a City player), was also against England six years later.

Davies was a contemporary of Billy Meredith, and had played alongside the 'Welsh Wizard' at Chirk. He won an unofficial cap against the Canadian Touring Side in 1891, and is the first player to represent any country whilst on the club's books.

WALSH, PAUL, born Plumstead, 1 October 1962. One of three players signed by Brian Horton at the end of the 1993/94 season (actual date 10 March), Paul Walsh shows as much enthusiasm today as he did when he made his debut for Charlton Athletic back in 1979.

He scored 24 goals in 85 (+2) league games for Charlton before a move to Luton in July 1982. At Luton he won the first of his five England caps (against Australia in Sydney on 12 June 1983), and maintained his scoring ratio with another 24 league goals, this time in just 80 (+2) games. He was also a member of the Luton side which relegated City in the last game of the 1982/83 season.

The PFA Young Player of the Year in 1984 moved to Liverpool in May that year, where he won a League Championship medal and played in finals of both the European and League Cups. Despite these successes, Walsh found it difficult to hold down a regular first team spot, and in February 1988 he moved to Tottenham for a fee of £500,000.

Internal disputes at White Hart Lane forced him to spend a short period on loan with Queen's Park Rangers before a £400,000 move to Portsmouth in 1992.

It looked as if Walsh might finish his career on the south coast (and indeed in the lower divisions), until Brian Horton's £700,000 swoop just two weeks before the transfer deadline. He made his debut for City in a 1–0 home defeat by Wimbledon on 12 March, and his efforts (and goals), when added to those of the other newcomers Uwe Rösler and Peter Beagrie, would steer City away from the relegation zone. He scored three times in his first three league outings of the 1994/95 season as well as a bizarre goal (with his face) away at Queen's Park Rangers. Given a second chance in the top flight, Walsh's enthusiasm will make sure he does not squander it lightly.

WALSH, WILLIAM, born Dublin, 31 May 1921. Wing-half William (Billy) Walsh was one of a rare breed of Irishmen, who was selected for both his native Republic, and for Northern Ireland. He played nine internationals for Eire and five for the North over a four year-period between 1946 and 1950.

Like many players of his era, however, he lost his best playing years to World War Two, after he joined City as an amateur on 5 May 1936 from neighbours United. His league debut came ten years later, on the opening day of the 1946/47 season (a 3–0 win at Leicester where he scored), although he had played in 240 wartime games for the Blues. Walsh was unlucky to miss out on a Second Division Championship medal that season, when the successful conversion of Albert Emptage from inside-forward to wing-half restricted him to only 13 league games.

He established a regular spot again the following season, and held his place for the next three campaigns, clocking up 114 league and cup appearances with just that one goal.

On 11 April 1951 he left Maine Road to become player/manager of Chelmsford City, and later managed Canterbury City and Grimsby Town.

WAR – CITY PLAYERS IN. The following City players were in the armed forces during World War Two:

ARMY – Bert Sprotson, Frank Swift, Sam Barkas, Eric Westwood, George Smith, Alex Herd, James Rudd, William Hogan, Harry Brunton, Thomas Wright, Sam Pearson, Edward McLeod, James Hope, Harvey Pritchard, Lewis Woodroffe.
NAVY – Albert Emptage, Joe Fagan.

RAF –   Louis Cardwell, Jackie Bray, Maurice Dunkley,
        Peter Doherty, manager Wilf Wild, Alfred
        Keeling, Wilfred Grant, David Davenport.
Other occupations – Les McDowall (draughtsman), Jimmy
        Heale (policeman), Billy Walsh
        (miner), Richard Neilson, John
        Milsom and Alex Roxburgh (firemen).

WAR – LOSSES. In World War One – George Brooks is believed to be the last British soldier to be killed in World War One. He died on Armistice Day 1918. At the time he was a Derby County player, but had played in three league games for the Blues in 1912.

Alex 'Sandy' Turnbull was a United player who had played for City from 1902 to 1906. He was killed at Arras on 3 May 1917. Frank 'Tabby' Booth died in Manchester Royal Infirmary from injuries sustained during World War One on 22 June 1919. He had two spells with City – 1902 to 1906, then in the 1911/1912 season, making a total of 98 league appearances.

Peter Gartland lost a leg in World War One in 1917. He had made one peacetime appearance for City, on Boxing Day 1914, a 2–1 win against Chelsea.

James Conlin was one of a new batch of players signed by City in the aftermath of the 1906 scandal. He played 161 league games for the Blues before a move to Birmingham City in January 1911. He was killed in Flanders on 23 June 1917 whilst serving with the Highland Light Infantry.

In World War Two – Alfred Keeling was signed by City in the summer of 1939 and played just one wartime league game before he was declared missing, presumed killed, as an RAF fighter pilot in December 1942.

WARD, MARK, born Prescot, 10 October 1962. Mark Ward arrived at Maine Road on 28 December 1989 as part of an exchange deal which saw City's Ian Bishop and Trevor Morley move to West Ham United.

Originally an apprentice with Everton, Ward moved to non-league Northwich Victoria where he played in an FA Trophy final at Wembley. In July 1983 he became an

Oldham Athletic player where he scored 12 times in 84 league appearances before a £250,000 move to Upton Park in August 1985.

Ward's debut for the Blues came in a 2–0 home victory over Millwall on 30 December 1989, and he played in the remaining 18 league games that season, scoring three times. All three goals came in 11 days in April 1990.

On 6 August 1991, after 15 goals in 67 league and cup appearances he rejoined Howard Kendall at Goodison Park along with teammate Alan Harper. Nowadays Ward is player/coach with Birmingham City.

WATSON, DAVE, born Stapleford, 5 October 1946. The holder of 65 England caps, centre-half Dave Watson began his playing career with Notts County in 1967.

The following year he moved to Rotherham United (managed by Tommy Docherty), where he played 121

Dave Watson – captain, Player of the Year and a key figure in the strong Blues sides of the late 70s (News Team International)

league games before a £100,000 move to Sunderland in December 1970.

At Sunderland he won an FA Cup Winners' medal (along with Dennis Tueart), in 1973, and in April the following year he won his first England cap in a goalless draw in Lisbon.

On 13 June 1975 Watson signed for the Blues, in a deal worth £275,000 and involving City's Jeff Clarke moving to Sunderland. Watson's first game in City's colours was the 1975/76 opener, a 3–0 home win against Norwich City. He was a Wembley winner again in 1976, finishing the League Cup final against Newcastle United with a badly cut head.

His sterling performances at the heart of the City defence earned him the club's Player of the Year award for 1976/77. He was a key member of the Blues' side that finished second in the First Division and was made captain for the 1977/78 season.

On 21 June 1979, Watson found himself a victim of manager Macolm Allison's clear-out policy and was sold to German side FC Werder Bremen. He returned to English football in October that year with Southampton, and later had spells with Stoke City, Derby County, Notts County, Vancouver Whitecaps and Fort Lauderdale Sun.

During his time at Maine Road, Dave Watson, one of City's best ever central defenders, scored six times in 185 league and cup appearances.

WEMBLEY. England's showcase football stadium, built in time for the famous 'White Horse' Cup final of 1923, has tragically not hosted a Manchester City game since the final of the Full Members' Cup on 23 March 1986.

Prior to this, the Blues have been visitors to the Twin Towers on 11 other occasions. Full details of these can be found under the headings FA CUP FINALS and FOOTBALL LEAGUE CUP. City fans need little reminding that the last successful Blues' visit to Wembley was on 28 February 1976, when Dennis Tueart's bicycle-kick won the League Cup final against Newcastle United.

WESTWOOD, ERIC, born Manchester, 25 September 1917. Eric Westwood began his career as an amateur with

Manchester United but moved to Maine Road on 13 November 1937. He made his debut for City in a 2–0 home victory over Tottenham Hotspur on 5 November 1938, and began a formidable full-back pairing with Bert Sprotson, who made his City debut in the same match.

Like Sprotson and many others, World War Two interrupted Westwood's playing career, and consequently he had to start all over again in 1946/47. During the war Westwood guested for five clubs, including Chelsea for whom he played in the 1944 War Cup final.

He missed just two league games in three seasons after the war, and continued to serve City up to the 1952/53 season, during which time he won a Second Division Championship medal and earned Football League and England B recognition.

On 10 June 1953, after 260 league appearances and five goals, the 35-year-old Westwood joined non-league Altrincham on a free transfer.

WHITE, DAVID, born Manchester, 30 October 1967. At the time of writing, David White is the last City player to represent England. His one and only cap (so far) came on 9 September 1992, as England lost 1–0 to Spain in Santander. (Prior to White, the last City player to play for England was Trevor Francis back in 1982, against Spain in Madrid.) White was a homegrown youngster, who signed as an apprentice professional on his 18th birthday, and was part of the very talented City youth team of 1986.

He made his debut for City (as a substitute) in a 1–0 defeat at Luton Town on 27 September 1986, and played 19 (+5) league games that season, which unfortunately ended in relegation. White was an ever-present in the next two Second Division seasons, and scored 19 times, including a hat-trick in the 10–1 mauling of Huddersfield Town.

A fast, attacking right-winger, White also had a spell leading the attack with Niall Quinn following the arrival of Mark Ward in December 1989. Statistics show his apparent preference for games at the end of the season. On 23 April 1991 he scored four in a 5–1 win at Aston Villa, and on 2

May the following year he scored three in a 5–2 win at Oldham Athletic.

On 22 December 1993, a run of bad form resulted in David White being transferred to Leeds United in an exchange deal for David Rocastle valued at £1.2 million. Even now a City supporter, David White had been top scorer for the Blues in his last two seasons with the club, and in total scored 95 times in 328 (+14) league and cup appearances.

WILD, WILF. Wilf Wild's association with the club lasted 30 years, from 1920 until his death in December 1950.

He was employed initially as assistant secretary, a post that remained his for four years until his promotion to secretary. In the spring of 1932, Wild found himself reponsible for team matters as well, when manager Peter Hodge returned to Leicester. Under Wild, City reached successive FA Cup finals, losing to Everton in 1933, but triumphing over Portsmouth the following year.

Players of the calibre of Frank Swift and Peter Doherty signed for the Blues during Wild's reign, which also saw them win the First Division Championship (for the first time in the club's history) in 1936/37. It is somewhat hard to believe that this same side would be relegated, despite scoring more goals than anyone else in the First Division, at the end of the 1937/38 season.

Wild did a splendid, although sometimes difficult, job to keep the club going throughout the hardships of World War Two, and he would eventually hand over control of team affairs to former player Sam Cowan in November 1946. At this point he reverted back to his former position of secretary, a job he was still performing until the time of his death.

WILLIAMS, ALEX, born Manchester, 13 November 1961. Born on the doorstep of Maine Road in Moss Side, Alex Williams was a solid, reliable goalkeeper who played 114 league games for the Blues in six years.

Signed as an apprentice professional from Manchester Boys on 11 July 1978, he made his debut on 14 March 1981 in a 2–1 home win over West Bromwich Albion. As understudy to Joe Corrigan, Williams played 20 league games over the next two seasons, before becoming the regular first choice keeper for the start of the 1984/85 season. That season saw City promoted, and Williams kept goal in all 42 league games, a feat he would emulate the following season. He kept a clean sheet in 33 of these 84 games, but found himself ousted by Eric Nixon in September 1985 after two successive 3–0 defeats. After two months there on loan, on 26 January 1987 he moved to Port Vale, where he played 35 league games. Today Alex Williams is an influential member of City's Football in the Community programme as Community Development Officer.

WILLIAMS, CHARLIE, born Welling, 19 November 1876. Charlie Williams joined City from Woolwich Arsenal on 5 June 1894 and proved a reliable servant over the next eight seasons, during which he would make 232 league and cup appearances and win a Second Division Championship medal.

He was described as a somewhat unorthodox goalkeeper who was considered unlucky at the time not to win England honours, although he did represent the Football League on one occasion. Williams is probably best remembered for reputedly scoring an unlikely goal for City in April 1900, when, on a windy day at Sunderland, his enormous clearance downfield bounced over the head of the Wearsiders' goalkeeper Doig and finished in the net.

He left Hyde Road in the summer of 1902 to move back to London and Tottenham Hotspur. He would later play for Norwich City and Brentford before managing French side Lille. Charlie Williams, perhaps the first goalkeeper ever to score a league goal, died in South America in 1952.

WILSON, CLIVE, born Manchester, 13 November 1961. A stylish player who can play in any position on the left side, Clive (christened Euclid) Wilson signed for City from Moss Side Amateurs on 5 December 1979. He began his career as a left-back, and it was in this position that he made his City debut, in front of more than 40,000 people on 28 December 1981, as the Blues beat Wolves 2–1 at Maine Road. Wilson found fierce competition for the number three shirt and made only another 13 league appearances over the next two seasons.

A move into midfield in City's promotion season of 1984/85 preceded his final breakthrough to the regular left-back slot for the start of the 1986/87 campaign.

On 19 March 1987, Wilson signed for Chelsea for £250,000, but the terms of the deal meant that he could stay at Maine Road on loan until the end of the season. This enabled him to play in all 42 league games of the season.

During his time at City, Wilson scored 11 goals in 124 (+2) league and cup appearances. In July 1990 he moved across London when Chelsea accepted £450,000 from Queen's Park Rangers for his services.

WOOSNAM, MAXWELL, born Liverpool, 6 September 1892. 'Gentleman' Max Woosnam was one of the most remarkable British sportsmen of all time. The son of a former Canon of Chester, he joined City from the Corinthians on 8 November 1919, and was the archetypal amateur of his era, always immaculately dressed and a gentleman in the truest sense of the word. He would often trot around the pitch carrying a handkerchief to enhance the image.

Woosnam went to Cambridge University where he won his Blue at soccer, tennis and golf, and was 12th man for the University cricket team.

He excelled at tennis, winning the 1920 Olympic Games Doubles with Turnbull, and in 1921 he won the Wimbledon title with R. Lycett. (The same year he was a runner-up in the Mixed Doubles final with Miss P.L. Howkins.) Amazingly he missed the start of the 1921/22 season for the Blues as he was away playing for the British Davies Cup team.

A powerful centre-half and captain for City and for England on his only international appearance (v Wales in 1922), Woosnam was one of the advocates of amateurs being allowed to play with professionals – and his stand against the Amateur Football Association over this matter only increased his popularity within the game. A broken leg sustained in a collision with a surrounding fence at Hyde Road curtailed his City career, and he moved on to Northwich Victoria in October 1925 after 93 league and cup appearances and four goals.

WORLD CUP FINAL STAGES – CITY PLAYERS IN.

Up to, and including USA '94, the following City players have represented their countries in the final stages of the World Cup:

Mexico	1970	Francis Lee and Colin Bell (England)
W. Germany	1974	Denis Law (Scotland)
Argentina	1978	Asa Hartford and Willie Donachie (Scotland)
Spain	1982	Trevor Francis (England) and Asa Hartford (Scotland)
Mexico	1986	Sammy McIlroy (Northern Ireland)
Italy	1990	Niall Quinn (Eire)
USA	1994	Terry Phelan and Alan Kernaghan (Eire)

WYNN, GEORGE, born Treflach, 14 October 1886. George Wynn was an industrious inside-forward who lost the best years of his career to World War One. He joined City from Wrexham on 23 April 1909, but had to wait until Christmas Day to make his debut. (City going down 2-0 at Bradford.)

Wynn became a regular over the rest of that 1909/10 season, and his 12 goals earned him a Second Division Championship medal as City clinched promotion. His performances caught the eye of the international selectors, and he made his Welsh debut against England in 1910.

The war intervened when Wynn was approaching his peak, and despite 30 games and nine goals in wartime football, he was sold to Coventry City for £300 on 20 November 1919, his best days effectively behind him.

His career at Hyde Road spanned ten years and included 127 league and cup appearances for City with 59 goals.

X = DRAWS. The most draws in one season for City is 18, from 42 league matches in 1993/94. The Blues finished 16th in the FA Premier League (just three points clear of relegation), and drew ten matches at Maine Road and eight on their travels.

X = XMAS DAY. Since 1891, City (or Ardwick) have played a total of 45 games on Xmas Day.

Their full record is:

P	W	D	L	F	A
45	15	11	19	78	86

Six of these matches were against Manchester United (or Newton Heath), with the spoils being shared evenly. City have won two, lost two and drawn two.

The last match to be played on Xmas Day was in 1957, when nearly 28,000 saw the Blues lose 2–1 at Burnley. Paddy Fagan scored City's goal that day, and was on the scoresheet 24 hours later when City won the return match 4–1 at Maine Road.

Barlow, Kirkman and Hayes scored the other goals in front of a crowd of 47,285.

As far as Xmas birthdays go, Stan Bowles was born on Xmas Eve 1948. Frank Swift 1913, Albert Emptage 1917 and Henry Travis 1911 (a reserve in 1930) were all born on Boxing Day.

The following players ran the risk of missing out on a birthday present, having been born on Xmas Day itself: Charlie Burgess 1901, Stephen Davidson 1953 (an apprentice in 1969) and John Moore 1919 (a guest player from Cardiff City in 1945/46).

Y

YOUNG, NEIL, born Manchester, 17 February 1944. Fallowfield-born Neil Young was a tall, graceful player with an explosive left-foot shot, who was an integral part of the Mercer/Allison team which swept the honours board during the late 60s and early 70s.

He had actually signed amateur for City on 15 May 1959, straight from school and Manchester Boys, and he made his debut on 25 November 1961 in a 2–1 defeat at Aston Villa. However, it was under Mercer and Allison that his career really blossomed. Perhaps his one weakness was that he was a poor header of the ball for such a big man, but he more than compensated in other ways. To see Young effortlessly glide past tackles before unleashing an unstoppable shot was a joy to behold, and his contribution to City's successes during that golden era was immense. (Did 'Nelly' ever fire a shot off target?)

He was leading scorer when the club won the Second Division Championship in 1965/66, and topped the scoring charts again two years later in the League Championship season. Many of his goals were priceless to the Blues.

He scored twice in the Championship decider at Newcastle, hit the 1969 FA Cup final winner against Leicester and two more in a rousing European Cup

Neil Young's left foot scored many spectacular and crucial goals for City during the golden era of the late 60s and early 70s
(News Team International)

Winners' Cup semi-final against FC Schalke. In the final of that competition, he scored the first against Gornik and was fouled for the penalty which clinched victory. Yet despite his goals, Young was never feted by the media as his more illustrious colleagues Lee, Bell and Summerbee were. His team-mates appreciated his worth however, as did the City fans who regarded him as an idol.

Young left Maine Road on 21 January 1972 in a £48,000 move to Preston, and later fell out with the club in a dispute over a richly deserved testimonial which was denied him. He refused to go near the ground for many years, but was finally welcomed back into the City family in 1994 after his former playing colleague and good friend Francis Lee had won his battle for control.

Neil Young's record of 409 (+3) league and cup

appearances and 107 goals bore witness to one of the most elegant players ever to grace City's books.

YOUNG PLAYER OF THE YEAR. Since 1988/89, the following young Blues have been voted by the fans as their Young Player of the Year:
1988/89   Ged Taggart
1989/90   Michael Hughes
1990/91   Adie Mike
1991/92   Mike Sheron
1992/93   David Kerr
1993/94   Rae Ingram
1994/95   Scott Thomas

YOUNGEST PLAYER. The youngest player to play a first team game for City is Glyn Pardoe.

He was just 15 years, 314 days old when he played against Birmingham City at Maine Road on 11 April 1962. Pardoe wore the number nine shirt as the Blues lost 4–1.

YOUTH CUP. Since the 1953/54 season, City have entered sides in the FA Youth Cup. To date, they have won the competition just once, in 1985/86 when Steve Redmond captained the side to victory 3–1 on aggregate over Manchester United.

They have reached the final on three other occasions:
1978/79 v Millwall   lost 2–0 on aggregate
1979/80 v Aston Villa   lost 3–2 on aggregate
1988/89 v Watford   lost 2–1 on aggregate.

Z

ZENITH DATA SYSTEMS CUP. – see under Full
Members' Cup.

BIBLIOGRAPHY

The following books were consulted at various times during the compiling of this encyclopedia:

Allison, Malcolm, *Soccer for Thinkers*, Pelham Books 1967

Allison, Malcolm, *Colours of My Life*, Everest Books 1975

Book, Tony, *Soccer; Skills of the Game*, Crowood Press 1989

Cawley, Steve and James, Gary, *The Pride of Manchester*, ACL Polar 1990

Creighton, John, *Manchester City; Moments to Remember*, Sigma Press 1992

Doyle, Mike, *Manchester City – My Team*, Souvenir Press 1977

Gardner, Peter, *The Manchester City Football Book 1*, Stanley Paul 1969

Gardner, Peter, *The Manchester City Football Book 2*, Stanley Paul 1970

Gardner, Peter, *The Manchester City Football Book 3*, Stanley Paul 1971

Gardner, Peter, *The Manchester City Football Book 4*, Stanley Paul 1972

Gardner, Peter, *The Manchester City Football Book 1978*, Stanley Paul 1978

Gardner, Peter, *The Manchester City Football Book 1979*, Stanley Paul 1979

Goble, Ray, *Manchester City: A Complete Record*, Breedon Books 1987 and 1993

Harding, John, *Billy Meredith*, Breedon Books 1985

James, Gary, *Football With a Smile: The Authorized Biography of Joe Mercer*, ACL Polar 1993

James, Gary, *From Maine Men to Banana Citizens*, Temple Press 1989

Johnson, Alec, *The Battle for Manchester City*, Mainstream 1994

Lee, Francis, *Soccer Round the World*, Arthur Barker 1970

Maddocks, John, *The Manchester City Quiz Book*, Mainstream 1988

M.C.F.C., *Official Handbooks Volumes 1 to 7*, ACL Polar

Marsh, Rodney, *Shooting to the Top*, Stanley Paul 1968

Oakes, Peter, *City – The Untold Story of a Club That Went Bananas*, Front Page Books 1989

Revie, Don, *Soccer's Happy Wanderer*, Museum Press 1955

Rowlands, Alan, *Trautmann: The Biography*, Breedon Books 1990

Swift, Frank, *Football From the Goalmouth*, Sporting Handbooks 1948

Thornton, Eric, *Manchester City – Meredith to Mercer and the FA Cup*, Robert Hale 1970

Trautmann, Bert, *Steppes to Wembley*, Robert Hale 1956

Ward, Andrew, *The Manchester City Story*, Breedon Books 1984

Whittell, Ian, *Manchester City Greats*, Sportsprint 1994

The following general reference books were also consulted:

Butler, Bryon, *The Football League 1888–1988*, Queen Anne Press 1987

Butler, Bryon, *The Official History of the Football Association*, Queen Anne Press 1991

Football Association, *Complete Guide to England Players Since 1945*, Stanley Paul 1993

Hugman, Barry, *FA Carling Premiership 1993/94 – The Players*, Williams 1993

Hugman, Barry, *Football League Players Records 1946 to 1992*, Williams 1992

Inglis, Simon, *The Football Grounds of Great Britain*, Collins 1987
Rothmans, *Football Yearbooks – Various*, Queen Anne Press
Turner, Dennis and White, Alex, *The Breedon Book of Football Managers*, Breedon Books 1993